BASIC INCOME *for* CANADIANS

The key to a **healthier, happier, more secure life** for all

EVELYN L. FORGET

James Lorimer & Company Ltd., Publishers

Toronto

James Lorimer & Company Ltd., Publishers acknowledges funding support from the Ontario Arts Council (OAC), an agency of the Government of Ontario. We acknowledge the support of the Canada Council for the Arts, which last year invested $153 million to bring the arts to Canadians throughout the country. This project has been made possible in part by the Government of Canada and with the support of the Ontario Media Development Corporation.

Cover design: Tyler Cleroux

Cover image: Shutterstock

Library and Archives Canada Cataloguing in Publication

Forget, Evelyn L. (Evelyn Louise), 1956-, author

    Basic income for Canadians : the key to a healthier, happier, more secure life for all / Evelyn L. Forget.

Includes bibliographical references and index.
Issued in print and electronic formats.
ISBN 978-1-4594-1350-4 (softcover).--ISBN 978-1-4594-1351-1 (EPUB)
    1. Guaranteed annual income--Canada. 2. Income distribution--Canada. 3. Income maintenance programs--Canada. 4. Poverty--Canada. 5. Canada--Social policy. 6. Economic security--Canada. 7. Social security--Canada. I. Title.
HC79.I5F68 2018   362.5'82 0971   C2018-904028-9
                                                   C2018-904029-7

James Lorimer & Company Ltd., Publishers
117 Peter Street, Suite 304
Toronto, ON, Canada
M5V 0M3
www.lorimer.ca

Printed and bound in Canada.

For Eric Richardson and the other participants of Mincome
who endured with kindness and good will and beyond all reason
the curiosity of reporters almost forty years later;

and,

For my mother, with love.

Courage, my friends: 'Tis not too late to build a better world.
– Tommy Douglas

Contents

LIST OF FIGURES

LIST OF TABLES

Introduction

In the summer of 2017, researchers in Ontario began to approach some people living in Hamilton to participate in a three-year experiment designed to test the feasibility and impact of a basic income guarantee. Over the next several months, participants in Hamilton, Thunder Bay and Lindsay slowly came forward and agreed to open their lives to researchers — to provide data on everything from their health, their work habits, their decision-making skills and the way they participate in society. As the first participants began to receive a basic income, some told their stories to journalists, sharing the satisfaction of buying their first new winter coat in years, or the pride associated with deciding to register in community college, or the simple satisfaction of providing a bedroom for their children. Then a provincial election brought the Progressive Conservative Party to power and, despite a campaign promise to see the experiment through, the Minister of Social Services announced the cancellation of the project in July 2018. Participants reported that they had only completed one survey when they began the program and had not been asked how their lives had changed when they began to receive a basic income.

Forty years ago, another Canadian basic income project drew to an end in somewhat similar circumstances. There were differences: Mincome ran its full course, despite the loss of political support that accompanied the election of the Progressive Conservative government provincially. Participants in Winnipeg, Dauphin and a few small rural communities in Manitoba received the stipend promised by the project and the project lasted long enough to collect data. However, the researchers were denied funding to analyze the 1,800 boxes of data collected, and they were put into storage in 1979. Almost a decade later, external researchers were able to access labour market data to show that a basic income had little effect on how many hours people worked. However, it took another thirty years to learn that the children of participants were more likely to complete high school, and that hospitalizations and visits to family doctors declined by 8.5 per cent among participants compared to similar people who did not receive a basic income.

The purpose of this book is to explore the meaning and feasibility of basic income in a Canadian context. How has the idea been discussed and made concrete in Canada, and how does our version of basic income differ from those proposed elsewhere? Why do we need a basic income in a country that already has a reasonably extensive social safety net? Who would benefit? Can we afford to offer all Canadians a basic income, and how would we pay for it? What about the social consequences? If we are all offered a basic income, why would anyone work for a living? Won't it just discourage the kind of independence and resilience we should be encouraging in our society?

This book is not a partisan tract. After reading the evidence, you can make up your own mind about whether basic income is a worthwhile investment and whether it is feasible. I've gathered the evidence that exists, identified what we know and the questions that remain to be answered. I've tried to correct some of the factual errors of both the critics and the proponents of basic income. In the end, I've convinced myself that a basic income of a very particular form is both necessary and affordable in Canada, and I've offered some suggestions about how we might proceed. My primary goal in this book, though, is to offer some clarity to a very necessary national conversation about how best to provide economic security in a rapidly changing and increasingly precarious world.

The idea of basic income — whether it's called basic income, basic income guarantee, guaranteed income, universal basic income, guaranteed annual income, unconditional cash transfer or something else — has gained a strong international foothold. Several high-income regions including Finland, the Netherlands, Barcelona, among others, have introduced experiments that are currently collecting data on the impact and feasibility of various designs. Several cities in Scotland and a few in the United States have firm plans for additional experiments, with more coming on board or just exploring possibilities. Low- and middle-income countries such as Malawi, India, Kenya and Namibia have been experimenting with unconditional and conditional cash-transfer programs for many years with funding from international aid agencies and the World Bank. Brazil's *Bolsa Familia*, while not a true basic income, raised many households out of dire poverty. Versions of basic income have informed, and continue to inform, social policy worldwide. Is there a role for basic income in Canada?

We begin, in Chapter 1, by defining basic income in its Canadian context and considering the many Canadians who would benefit. The one fundamental defining characteristic of a basic income of any type is that it must be unconditional. There is no requirement to work or seek work, or to have worked a certain number of hours in the recent past; people must be free to decide how to use their time, whether that means working for pay, volunteering, training for a new job, starting a new business, creating art or doing anything else they choose. This reduces the need for a costly and intrusive bureaucracy to ensure that people comply with an extensive list of regulations. One further characteristic is consistent with the way basic income is being discussed in Canada: basic income is not a replacement for all other social expenditure. We still require basic public infrastructure like transport and water, public health insurance and education. Some people with disabilities still require additional supports beyond income, and people with particular challenges, such as precariously housed people with mental health issues, still require dedicated programs that have been shown to be effective. Basic income is not designed to meet the specific needs of these relatively small numbers of Canadians. Rather, basic income can provide income security for people who may not now require income support, but who are as vulnerable to economic downturns and health challenges as anybody else, and it can bolster the incomes of the very many people whose greatest need is not more special programs or more paperwork to complete, but simply access to money that would allow them to make better decisions for their families. These families, whether they currently work and earn too little to support themselves or receive income support from the provinces, deserve incomes adequate to meet modest needs delivered with dignity.

Worldwide, basic income takes two forms. One is universal: everyone, by virtue of residence or citizenship, receives the same amount of money from the state. This is normally a taxable benefit, so high-income individuals would pay some portion of the benefit back to the state through higher tax payments. The second form, which is the only version that has been discussed in detail in Canada, is a benefit that is based on financial need. This version of basic income works like a tax credit: an individual with no other income would receive the full benefit, which is tax-free. As income from other sources increases, the benefit gradually declines. In the Ontario experiment, an individual living on his or her own with no income would have received a basic income of almost $17,000 a year. If she chose to work and earned $100, her benefit would decline by $50. This means that no individual with an income above $34,000 would receive any support from a basic income. These are two very different versions of basic income.

This book takes the position, as does virtually all of the policy conversation in Canada, that a basic income based on financial need is better for Canada. A program that is based on financial need is very similar to other programs we already have in place, such as the Canada Child Benefit, which is, for all intents and purposes, a basic income for families with dependent children. A basic income based on financial need will also cost taxpayers *much* less than a universal basic income — indeed, as we will see in Chapter 9, the Parliamentary Budget Office estimates the net cost of a national rollout of the Ontario scheme at approximately the same amount that we currently spend for our Canada Child Benefit, without taking into account potential savings from other social programs. It is financially feasible.

Chapter 2 — "Rediscovering Mincome" — takes us back in time to the 1970s, when Canada ran a three-year basic income experiment in Manitoba that served as the inspiration for Ontario's design. In some ways, Mincome represents a cautionary tale: it was cost-shared by the provincial and federal governments, and changes in governments meant that a great deal of data was collected, but little analysis was completed before the experiment ended and the data was put into storage. Some economists used part of the data in the 1980s to determine whether Winnipeg residents had reduced the number of hours they worked when they were offered a basic income. Spoiler alert! Most hadn't, and the total number of worked hours had fallen by very little. However, the vast social surveys conducted, as well as the entire archive from the town of Dauphin — one of three sites where the project was implemented — remained unanalyzed. Many years later, I went back to the Dauphin archive and found that a town that benefited from a basic income saw significant increases in its high school completion rate and, even more surprising, people were much less likely to be hospitalized when they received a basic income. Mental health was especially affected. Chapter 3 explores the relationships between income, health and the costs of delivering health care.

Chapters 4 and 5 look at the relationship between work and basic income. Are we heading into a future in which artificial intelligence and robots will reduce the need for human labour, as many in Silicon Valley suggest, or is our way of life dependent on squeezing ever more productivity out of a shrinking labour force? Why do people work anyway, and how many would work less if they could?

Chapters 6 and 7 recognize that a basic income will have very different effects on different people. We look at the potential implications for women, Indigenous people, newcomers, people of colour, people with disabilities and youth. Chapter 8 examines some of the more extravagant fears and hopes associated with discussions of basic income. Chapter 9 demonstrates the financial feasibility of a targeted basic income, and Chapter 10 addresses the complexity of policy change in a federal system and explores a gradual implementation of basic income.

Basic income is not a utopian project. Canadians are a practical people, not easily seduced by impossible dreams. A targeted basic income is feasible, and its affordability has been assessed by no less an authority than the Parliamentary Budget Office. It is, however, not costless. It is a significant investment in the kind of society we want to build. Canadians are also people who value fairness, and who recognize that unexpected things sometimes happen, and people deserve second chances. A basic income provides insurance that, no matter what happens, we will all have the opportunity to recover and try again.

Chapter 1
A Basic Income Guarantee for Canada

The 2008 financial meltdown shocked many of us living in high-income countries like Canada. Those with investments watched as the value of their assets declined. As the fallout spread through the economy, some people who had been working in what they thought were good jobs found themselves out of work. In some cases, the firms that they had counted on to pay their pensions were facing bankruptcy with underfunded pension plans. People working in the resource sector were let go by firms facing softer markets for their products. In the manufacturing sector, the already established trend toward producing more output with less labour offered fewer employment options. Young people with good job skills and strong degrees struggled to find work, or even to secure an internship that might lead to a permanent job.

The financial shock reminded many of us that the middle-class lives we've built for ourselves are really very fragile. No one is immune to unexpected economic events. Even people who've done everything right — earned good work skills, worked hard to find a job with good pay and benefits, saved for their children's education and invested for their own futures — can watch with little recourse as their lives unravel. Canadians have been fortunate. Since 2008, our economy has largely recovered, although not everyone has shared equally in the economic gains. However, many of us remember the vulnerability and helplessness that we felt in 2008. We also face other life events that we cannot control; we will get sick and we will have accidents, as will our children, partners and parents. Sometimes, we recover quickly and our own savings allow us to cope with the unexpected. Other times, the setback is permanent and we have no choice but to realize that our life is not going to unfold the way we had planned.

Whatever our current financial situation, no one who lived through the recession sparked by the 2008 financial crisis will ever feel quite as invulnerable as they did before 2008. Economic insecurity is the defining characteristic of our age, and it is not synonymous with poverty. Persistent poverty is a problem in Canada, but so too is the insecurity of those who are not now poor, but who may become so at a moment's notice. People without enough resources to meet modest needs with dignity require a secure, adequate and predictable income. Those who are economically insecure need an insurance policy to protect them against the risk of poverty and loss. A basic income is designed to meet both needs.

In 2016, the federal government introduced the Canada Child Benefit "to strengthen the middle class and help those working to join it."[1] As of 2018, more than 90 per cent of families with children under eighteen were receiving at least partial benefits. This builds on a decision made many years ago in Canada to introduce the Guaranteed Income Supplement (GIS) to augment Old Age Security (OAS) pensions for low-income Canadians over age sixty-five. Neither program is perfect; certainly benefits for older Canadians could be increased, and all benefits should be adjusted annually for the cost of living. However, the design of both programs is sound and delivers to families with children under eighteen and to those over sixty-five a guarantee that they will have access to a predictable income sufficient to meet their basic needs.

Adult Canadians without dependent children have no such guarantee. Take for example:

Sharma, who works two jobs to make ends meet. Trained as an engineer in Nepal, he immigrated to Canada ten years ago. He earned his millwright certificate and quickly found a series of full-time jobs with different employers. Three years ago, he was laid off and took a part-time job paying $18 an hour as a security guard. Some months he gets full-time hours, but often he gets fewer. His wife works part-time at Costco, and together the family can just cover rent. Recently, he took a second part-time job and supplements his income by delivering food through *Skip the Dishes* (an online platform) that lets him choose when and how much he works. He hopes that one day his wife might find a higher-paying job that would let him become accredited as an engineer in Canada;

Debbie, who earned her PhD in anthropology five years ago and lives in a large Canadian city. She delivers courses for up to 200 students each at three different universities and earns less than $8,000 per course. Most terms, she can find one or two (sometimes three) courses and shuttles between employers, but she has no job security, no sick leave and no benefits. She doesn't even have an office in which to meet with students. Three times a year, she must reapply and wait for job offers. She might be offered a course with little notice, or a course might be cancelled with no compensation two weeks before term begins if enrollments are deemed "too low" by the university administration. Every year she spends as an itinerant lecturer means less time to publish the articles and apply for the grants that might make her eligible for full-time, permanent employment as a professor. She wonders how she can afford to have a child before she runs out of time. The stress is mounting;

Allen, who was a fifty-four-year-old financial advisor for a large firm. His company was acquired by a rival and he, along with most of his colleagues, was offered a severance package. He sheltered as much as he could in his RRSP and went to work to find a new job. He'd never been unemployed and expected that his skills would be in high demand. When he had no offers from the financial industry, he worked with an employment counselor to identify his transferable skills and sent résumés for management and sales positions. All the while, his savings paid the mortgage on his house, contributed to his children's activities and covered the other costs incurred by his family. His wife found a part-time job and Allen lowered his expectations. He ultimately found a new contract position with a small start-up firm. The chronic financial stress began to affect his health, and Allen had a stroke that resulted in several weeks of hospitalization and rehabilitation. He worked hard to recover, but his job was gone when he was ready to return. His house is for sale, his children are no longer in dance and hockey, and his wife is looking for additional work. Allen has been spending his retirement savings — assets that make him ineligible for income assistance. Yet he worries that his savings will not stretch to cover his needs since he began withdrawing a decade earlier than planned and will have little opportunity to recover before retirement even if he does find a new job;

Dylan, who has two master's degrees — one in economics and one in disability studies. He has good programming skills and writes well. Despite his skill set, he has been unable to find permanent work since his graduation. For the past ten years, he has worked at reasonably well-paying jobs in the health care sector, but always on temporary contracts with no pension and few benefits. There is never a guarantee that his contract will be renewed, or even a suggestion that it might one day lead to a permanent position;

Lorelei, who left her job as a housekeeper in a hotel at the age of sixty to spend more time with her twenty-four-year-old daughter, Susan, who has mental health challenges that have made it hard for her to hold a job. Susan's mental health has declined to the point that she depends on her single mother to help her with routine tasks, and Lorelei is not comfortable leaving Susan alone while she works. Susan is on the waitlist for housing and programming alternatives. She just qualified for provincial disability support. Each month Lorelei and Susan work through the mountain of paperwork required. Late reports and missed appointments, both of which happen too frequently because of Susan's mental health challenges, result in delayed or denied payments. Lorelei has no retirement savings and little entitlement to retirement benefits under the Canada Pension Plan because of her erratic work history; and

Pete, who lives in Ontario and until recently worked at a factory job manufacturing automobile parts. He had a decent salary and good benefits through his union. The factory is still there — producing and selling more than ever. However, the workers that used to make it run are no longer so numerous. To compete internationally, the firm decided that costs had to fall. Some of the work is now done outside the country, and most of what is done in Canada is heavily automated. Workers have been replaced by machines. The investment paid off for the owners, but guys like Pete find themselves living in small towns with houses that aren't appreciating in value the way they do in Toronto, and a community that is aging as young people leave to find work. The best he has been able to find is a part-time retail job that guarantees him far less than he used to make but offers him the opportunity to make commissions. He has always worked hard, but never knowing how much he might bring home is stressful.

None of these individuals has been persistently "poor." You wouldn't see them panhandling or sleeping rough. But they are all, for various reasons, experiencing economic insecurity. A basic income guarantee would act as a top-up in harder times as well as serve as a valuable insurance policy — a promise that no matter what, the floor won't fall out from beneath their feet.

What Is Basic Income?
A basic income:

- Provides insurance against income insecurity for all of us. Anyone can lose the trappings of a middle-class life when the economy implodes or when their health fails. Sometimes the loss is temporary; other times, recovery is challenging.

- Addresses financial need, whether temporary or permanent, with dignity. Most people facing income insecurity are no different from the schoolteachers, factory workers, police officers, lawyers or hairdressers who are still working. They are ordinary people, just like the rest of us, who have had some bad luck or made some bad decisions.

- Invests in people when they need help, so that taxpayers don't have to pay higher costs later for the avoidable consequences of poverty. Other social programs pay the price when income insecurity is not addressed. Health care costs soar with the stress of uncertainty. Property crime increases along with poverty and inequality. Special education and child services are called in when children fall behind or develop behavioural problems because they change schools too often when their parents struggle to pay the rent.

A basic income promises every working-age adult an income suffi-cient to meet basic needs and live a decent life. No one is asked to demonstrate that they've looked for a job or participated in programs designed to make them more employable.

In Canada, basic income has most often been discussed as a non-taxable benefit targeted toward low-income people. Financial support is reduced gradually as other income increases, in much the same way that the Canada Child Benefit operates.[2] This Canadian version of basic income differs from some other versions in which everyone, rich or poor, receives the same taxable payment each month.[3]

Depending on its design, basic income might replace provincial income assistance (what most people might call welfare or social assis-tance, depending on which province they live in) and some federal and/ or provincial tax benefits, but it will not replace all social programs. We still require public health care, education and other social supports. Employment Insurance is paid for by employers and workers; it offers temporary relief for people facing short-term unemployment and serves a useful economic purpose. The Canada Pension Plan is a social insur-ance plan for the retired and some people with disabilities financed by contributions from workers and employers; it provides useful benefits and should be retained. Basic income would become part of the social safety net rather than a replacement for it.

In 2018, many governments around the world, including the Ontario provincial government, were contemplating or implementing basic income experiments designed to test the concept. The Ontario project was prematurely cancelled by a new government before it yielded any results, but experiments elsewhere continue. However, the idea itself has a very long history, and there have already been several basic income experi-ments in low, medium and high-income countries around the world.[4] We also have some experience with a basic income in Canada. In the 1970s, we conducted a basic income experiment called Mincome in the prov-ince of Manitoba that offered participants a basic income for three years. It, too, was stopped by government edict before a final analysis could be completed. Fortunately, the persistence of external researchers over the following decades has begun to reveal how well Mincome worked to improve mental and physical health, educational outcomes and social well-being without causing people to work less as had been feared.

We already have some programs that are, in effect, basic incomes for some groups of people. The Canada Child Benefit is a form of basic income for families with children under age eighteen, and the Old Age Security pension in combination with the Guaranteed Income Supplement is a form of basic income for those over sixty-five. The current debate in Canada is about whether a basic income should also be offered to working-age adults. A basic income for Canada is neither impossibly utopian nor outrageously expensive. We can afford to provide Canadians with a basic income. Choosing to do so is simply a matter of deciding what kind of a society we want to live in.

Provincial Income Assistance Is Not a Basic Income

Some people who have never had to depend on income assistance might wonder why a basic income is necessary in Canada. Each Canadian province already has its own system of income assistance, sometimes called social assistance or welfare, designed as a program of last resort for working-age adults between eighteen and sixty-four. However, in each case, provincial income assistance is governed by regulations that exclude many people who would benefit from a basic income. Sharma, Debbie and Dylan do not qualify for provincial income assistance because they are working. Allen does not qualify because he has investments and property that must be sold to support his family before he can apply. Pete might one day qualify, after he has run through most of his savings and sold any assets like a snowmobile, a boat or a car worth more than fifteen thousand dollars. Lorelei receives provincial income assistance, and Susan receives provincial disability support, but their incomes are neither secure nor unconditional, nor are they delivered in a way that allows them to preserve their self-respect.

David Northcott, the longtime director of Winnipeg Harvest Food Bank, loves to tell the story of "Big Bill" Adamson. Big Bill sorted potatoes at Winnipeg Harvest and, like many of the volunteers at the food bank, he was also a client. He lived in a tiny residential hotel room downtown. He wore all his clothes all the time, so no one would steal them. He often struggled with hygiene because the shared shower was broken or otherwise unusable. One day, he came to work and looked different. He was cleaner and wasn't wearing all his clothes. What had brought about the change? Big Bill had had a birthday. The day he turned sixty-five, he was eligible for Old Age Security and the Guaranteed Income Supplement for seniors and no longer dependent on provincial income assistance. Overnight, his income doubled. He rented a modest apartment with its own bathroom, and he had access to cooking facilities for the first time. Instead of lining up for hours to eat dinner at a downtown charity, or buying ready-made food to eat from the package, he could go to a grocery store and buy several cans of beans or chili at a time and prepare his own dinner in his own apartment.

Seniors in need of income support in Canada are treated very differently than adults of working age. Seniors are entitled to significantly more money, and the money they receive is unconditional; everyone who meets the income threshold is entitled to receive support. Seniors do not have to convince a caseworker that they are actively seeking work or registered in a program to prepare them for work. They are not subject to periodic reviews or asked to document their needs. They do not have to report where they live and who they live with, and changes in their circumstances are their own business.

By contrast, adults under age sixty-five who have no other means of support can apply for income assistance. In each case, the province tries to encourage recipients to find paid employment or someone else to support them by imposing strict eligibility requirements and employing caseworkers whose job is to identify recipients who do not qualify.

To apply for income assistance, an applicant must provide documentation that includes their social insurance number, provincial health card and birth certificate. They must document their income, assets and debt by providing bank statements and income tax forms. Age, education, immigration status, past employment, housing costs and the number of people in the family will be documented. A worker can arrive at any time during normal business hours, without notice, and ask to inspect an applicant's home. They can verify the information provided by contacting the bank and the Canada Revenue Agency. In most provinces, a recipient can have no more than five thousand dollars in assets.[5]

The amount of support provided varies by family size and province. A single adult in Ontario, for example, will be eligible for a maximum shelter allowance of $384 and a basic needs allowance of $337, for a total of $721 per month. A family of two adults will receive an additional $397 per month. Recipients will also receive extended health benefits that pay for dental, vision, drugs, hearing and other related costs. Some might also be eligible for some federal and provincial refundable tax credits, if they apply. Tax credits are not automatic. The total of these benefits is still considerably less than the minimum monthly income of $1,459.97 that a single adult can receive, without condition, from Old Age Security and the Guaranteed Income Supplement the moment he or she turns sixty-five.

To continue receiving provincial income assistance, recipients have a number of obligations. Everyone must meet with his or her caseworker every three months and take part in approved activities designed to help them find a job. However, a recipient cannot register in an educational program without the explicit consent of his or her caseworker. Recipients must report any income they receive and keep receipts and statements to document income, assets and expenses. Recipients are required to report any changes in circumstances, such as a new job, opening or closing a bank account, having a baby, moving, or having a partner move in. Recipients are required to obtain any other income or support they are entitled to, including child support from previous partners. Recipients are required to provide any document or information their worker requests. If they do not comply, they may be disqualified or have their benefits reduced. If they do not meet the deadline for submitting requested documents, their next payment may be delayed or reduced.

If a recipient takes a job while on income assistance in Ontario, they are allowed to earn two hundred dollars per month with no penalty. When earnings exceed this, benefits are reduced by fifty cents for every dollar earned. This is one of the most generous treatments of employment income in Canada, and it was intended to encourage people to become independent of income assistance. Most provinces continue to reduce benefits on a dollar-for-dollar basis after a small allowance. However, many people who rely on income assistance in Ontario still find it difficult to extract themselves from the program because they may lose their extended health benefits. Most low-income workers are not eligible to receive income assistance because they cannot qualify under the rigid regulations of the system. They might own a vehicle worth more than fifteen thousand dollars, or they might not be prepared to pursue a former partner for child support, or they may simply be unwilling to submit to the intrusion into their personal lives that the system requires.

Provincial income assistance across Canada pays too little to allow recipients to live adequately. It relies on caseworkers to interpret a complex system of regulations, which means that recipients can never know with certainty how much they are entitled to receive, or when they will receive it. Moreover, provincial income assistance cannot deal seamlessly with low-waged working people and most of the people who live in poverty in this country are employed. Provincial income assistance, based as it is on regulation and surveillance, cannot be other than intrusive and stigmatizing. It works by taking away from recipients the ability to decide for themselves how to live their lives and how to spend their money.

Fewer than 2 per cent of Canadians are both living in poverty and aged sixty-five or over, because Old Age Security and the Guaranteed Income Supplement together are effective income support schemes. Some younger families and individuals who might benefit from a basic income are already recipients of provincial income assistance. These families, who represent about 5.1 per cent of Canadians, will benefit from basic income primarily because it is a more efficient, more generous and less stigmatizing program that does not depend on the discretion of caseworkers. A basic income will continue to support these families as they transition from dependence to independence in the labour market.

The additional benefits currently tied to income assistance in many provinces, such as extended health benefits, should be available to all Canadians based on level of income rather than source of income. Manitoba and Saskatchewan currently offer pharmacare to low-income working people as well as to those receiving income assistance; support for prescription drugs in these two provinces is based on the level of income a family receives, rather than its source. Dental, mobility, vision and hearing care and appliances, along with other similar supports, could be offered, alongside a basic income, based on level of income. This would extend support to those who work for low wages and elimi-nate the risk that discourages people who currently receive income assistance or disability support from trying to work.

Figure 1.1   Who is Living in Poverty in Canada?

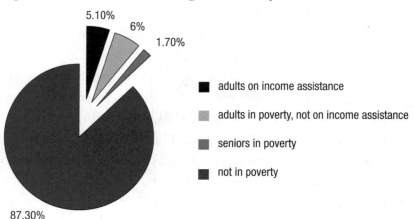

Note: Due to rounding the numbers add to 100.1 per cent.

Source: John Stapleton, "A Basic Income and Canada's Income Security System," Open Policy Institute. Presented in Hamilton, November 23, 2016.[6] Based on the After-Tax Low Income Measure. openpolicyontario.com/presentations/

The biggest flaw of existing provincial income assistance, however, is that it offers no income support at all to the largest group of poor Canadians: low-income working people. There are more working Canadians living in poverty than there are income assistance recipients. Six per cent of Canadian adults rely on the labour market for support yet still earn too little to lift themselves out of poverty. There are few Canadian programs in place to help low-income working people. The federal GST credit and the Canada Workers Benefit (formerly known as the Working Income Tax Benefit) are helpful but too small to be of much use. Moreover, the complexity of applying for these benefits dissuades many who are eligible. Labour legislation and mandated increases to minimum wage help, but neither ensures that a low-waged worker will be employed enough hours to earn a decent living.

The 2016 census showed that only 49.8 per cent of those in their peak working years (twenty-five to fifty-four) were in full-time, full-year work, although 87 per cent of these people were in the labour market. While wage growth among the lowest-paid workers has increased, largely due to higher minimum wages imposed by policy, those in the next-lowest wage categories have not seen commensurate increases. More Canadians are now employed at lower wages than ever before, with 61 per cent of Canadians, and 54 per cent of those between twenty-five and fifty-four, now earning less than the average wage.[7] These changes seem to be a permanent feature of the changing economy.

A basic income is a better way of dealing with poverty than provincial income assistance because it offers a stable, predictable income to the working poor as well as those who currently receive income assistance. It does not penalize those who try to move into the labour market by taking away other benefits associated with income assistance. It is not punitive; the benefit an individual will receive does not depend on the discretion of a frontline worker.

A Basic Income Is More than an Antipoverty Program

A basic income also provides insurance for those of us who currently earn a decent living in the labour market. Universal health insurance is among the most popular programs that exist in Canada, not because we all make equal use of it, but because we can all imagine circumstances in which we might need help. A basic income is similar; even those of us who currently hold good, solid, middle-class jobs can no longer assume that we will do so for the rest of our working lives. We have always been vulnerable to poor health and accidents that force many of us to stop working before we are old enough to receive pensions. But the changing economy has introduced new kinds of job insecurity.

Over the past half century, the labour market has changed in dramatic ways. If we are just entering the labour force, we know that we will be retraining, probably more than once, for jobs that we cannot yet imagine. If we are older, we recognize the effort that younger family members have gone through to find their first jobs and establish themselves in the labour market. There are far fewer lifetime jobs with benefits, decent wages and union protection. There are many more contingent jobs — short-term contracts, self-employment and permanent part-time — and young workers are the most vulnerable. However, they are not alone. Older workers displaced from jobs in the resource or manufacturing sectors increasingly find that their skills are not enough for them to find employment similar to the jobs they left behind. As factories and mines close, big box stores open. New opportunities pay lower wages and offer fewer benefits. Many costs that used to be associated with employing labour, such as the provision of a pension and benefits such as health care, have been shifted to taxpayers.

The number of contingent workers in Canada has grown from 4.8 million in 1997 to 6.1 million in 2015. Almost one-third of Canadian jobs are for contingent workers, yet temporary positions pay 30 per cent less on average than permanent positions, and only 24 per cent of Canadian workers are covered by private sector pension plans.[8]

A basic income can address the problems associated with the growth of precarious employment. We used to think we could easily distinguish between workers, retirees, people facing short-term unemployment, people not in the workforce, students and people with disabilities. Consequently, we have Employment Insurance for the short-term unemployed, Disability Support for people with disabilities, special programs for students, Old Age Security, the Guaranteed Income Supplement and the Canada Pension Plan for the retired and income assistance for people not in the workforce. All of these programs are associated with strictly enforced eligibility criteria to make sure that individuals access the correct program for their needs. The growth of precarious employment, however, makes these distinctions almost meaningless. Workers may be trying to support families with part-time jobs when they would prefer full-time work that is not available to them, or they may be subsisting between short-term contracts. People who want to work might find themselves effectively "retired" many years before they would like to be. Some people with disabilities, especially mental health and other invisible disabilities, are rejected when they apply to programs for people with disabilities yet are still unable to find and keep jobs in standard workplaces unwilling or unable to accommodate their needs. Workers have childcare and senior care responsibilities along with job responsibilities. Many unemployed people cannot access Employment Insurance because their previous work did not allow them to amass the hours required for eligibility. People on income assistance would often like to work but fear the loss of drug or extended health benefits that they or their family members rely on and receive as part of their income assistance.

A basic income would bridge the gap between many of these programs, supplementing the incomes of those who retire too early because their jobs end, and filling gaps between employment for those who make do with short-term contracts. It would support those unable to work because of the illness or disability of a family member or because of their own health challenges. It would supplement the incomes of low-waged workers, especially young people struggling to find permanent work in a changing economy, and subsidize individuals who choose to engage in job training or other education. One of the most important characteristics of basic income is that recipients are not required to seek approval to spend their money or their time in particular ways. They have the freedom to use their resources in ways that best meet the needs of their families.

How Do We Expect a Basic Income to Make Canadians Better Off?

A basic income that effectively addresses the issues of poverty and economic insecurity will have other consequences for Canadian society. Income affects our sense of self and the opportunities we have to consume, to invest, to save and to give, and each of these affects our health, our social well-being, our ability to parent, our education and our ability to withstand adversity.

Health and Well-Being

Our health care system does a reasonable job of addressing illness, but it does little to keep people well. Many of the people being treated at inner-city clinics and busy hospital Emergency Departments are there because of the lives they have lived. Our health is affected by our income, the social support we can rely on, our social status, our education, the social and physical conditions in which we work and live, our personal health practices and coping skills and the opportunities we had as children. These social determinants of health are all interrelated, but income is fundamental to our lives. It affects the kind of housing and neighbourhoods we live in and our ability to access education and to offer opportunities to our children.

Income also affects our ability to access health care not provided by the province or federal government. While hospital services and visits to family doctors are routinely available to all Canadians, dental work and prescription medications are not. Some provinces provide means-tested pharmaceutical coverage for all adults, but others do not. People who currently depend on provincial income assistance have access to extended health care, and those who work at good jobs have access to these services through their benefits packages at work, but people who work part time and on short-term contracts often have no coverage for such fundamental needs. The implications go beyond the suffering associated with unmet health needs. Dental health, for example, is one of the informal markers of social status in our society. People with bad teeth present poorly in job interviews and are often not hired into higher-level positions that require interaction with the public. This makes it harder to escape from poverty and to become self-supporting. People with inadequate pharmaceutical coverage miss time at work and are sometimes hospitalized because they cannot adequately control their health conditions.

Education and Training

In a rapidly evolving labour market, continuing education is fundamental. A basic income can be especially important at three times in our lives. Young children, growing up in households with adequate incomes, can go to school secure and well fed. Educational outcomes improve when families with adequate incomes move less often, and children can continue in the same school. As adolescents, children in families with adequate incomes and less parental stress may be less vulnerable to neighbourhood risk factors associated with leaving school early. They may feel less pressure to become independent and self-supporting if their parents have the resources to support them. Finally, for adults a basic income can provide the resources necessary to take time out of the labour market to access further training.

The ability to use a basic income to fund retraining makes it possible to get a better job. Instead of a lifetime of working at minimum wage or near–minimum wage jobs, an individual with a basic income can retrain to meet the changing demands of the labour market. This makes it possible to compete for better-paid permanent jobs with benefits instead of dealing with the income insecurity associated with low-waged, part-time work. Basic income provides a structure that supports individuals as they work to better their conditions; it is not simply a source of short-term support for people mired in inadequate work.

Financial Resilience

A basic income does more than allow people to meet their day-to-day needs for survival. People can count on receiving their basic income without worrying about how a caseworker will choose to interpret and apply a set of confusing and inconsistent regulations. They know how much they will receive and when it will appear in their bank accounts. While these seem like small matters to many of us, it is almost impossible to plan and to save if you cannot rely on an adequate, dependable, predictable income. When you might be penalized for breaking a regulation you didn't know about, it seems reasonable to spend whatever money you receive as soon as it appears in your account for fear that it might be snatched back. When regulations associated with provincial income assistance limit the amount of assets you can hold, it makes little sense to save for the future. Why save for unexpected (or even expected) needs when you know there might be funding available through the discretion of a caseworker if you can demonstrate need? Provincial income assistance is a system predicated on crisis. It was established to respond to crisis, and it perpetuates a situation where a recipient is always on the edge of crisis.

By contrast, a predictable basic income allows individuals to make decisions about how to allocate their money and how to save for future purchases or unexpected events. Having an adequate, predictable income allows people to take control of their own lives. It allows people to make choices about how they will live, and with the ability to choose comes autonomy and self-respect.

Healthy Labour Market Attachment and Creativity

At the heart of much of the controversy associated with basic income is the fear that a basic income will free workers to work less or not at all. But there are many people who do important work outside the traditional labour market. Artists and actors rarely earn enough to pay the rent without a side job in a café or elsewhere. Many entrepreneurs face a long period before their new enterprise generates enough income to pay a salary. Other people do not work for pay but spend much of their time working for their families and communities. All of these activities contribute to the richness of the society in which we live.

If some people do choose to spend less time in paid work, at least some will contribute to our social well-being. Even those who choose to spend less time working and more time in traditional leisure activities might ultimately be more productive in the labour market as a result of the time away from work. Basic income encourages us, among other things, to have a broader conversation about the meaning of work in our lives.

Responsible Citizenship

The most important consequence of basic income is that it will allow all Canadians to decide for themselves how to live their lives without the coercion of grinding poverty, the stress of income insecurity or the humiliation associated with income assistance. It allows each of us the basic resources we require to participate in our society. We can register our child in theatre or hockey. We can enjoy the small pleasures of going to a coffee shop or a neighbourhood pub without worrying about the few dollars involved. We may find time to volunteer in our communities or to help our neighbours and family members who require additional support. All of us will have the same opportunities to make our own decisions and to live with the consequences of those decisions.

Chapter 2
Rediscovering Mincome

In 1974, I was a first-year student at Glendon College in Toronto intending to major in psychology. I found myself registered in an economics class, almost by accident, and vowed to make the best of what I expected to be a rather boring term. I was interested in people — not interest rates and tax expenditures! It was a time of optimism and social change, and, like many of my classmates, I wanted to help make the world a little more just and the lives of ordinary people a little bit easier. I didn't expect economics to have much to say about the world I'd grown up in.

During the course of that year, and under the mentorship of an extraordinary professor named Ian McDonald, I came to understand my own relationship to money. I was the oldest of three children, and my father died when I was twelve. My mother had few job skills; like many women of her generation, she never expected to have to support a family on her own. She raised us, first on Mother's Allowance and later through a series of low-skilled and not particularly well-paid jobs. I learned very quickly how important money is, and how vulnerable anyone becomes when they have no money of their own. People with money have choices and opportunities that others don't have. I knew that my widowed mother struggled financially to support three young children. However, I had the opportunity to complete high school because my mother chose to allow me to live at home even when I was old enough to work. I could make the choice to go to college, unlike most of my friends, because I was fortunate enough to receive a scholarship. The availability of money then, and for many years of schooling to come, gave me a life that my parents couldn't have imagined, and that most of my friends didn't share.

The year 1974 was important on many levels. Professor McDonald told a story about an experiment that was just being set up in Western Canada called Mincome that would, he was convinced, transform the way we delivered social programs in Canada. With charts and graphs, he showed us how the current system of income assistance created walls that prevented people from becoming independent; if they earned a little money, they lost not only their welfare cheque but also all the benefits, such as drug and dental care, that accompanied income assistance. He explained that working was no guarantee against poverty; low-waged workers struggled to provide for themselves and their families. He used the tools of economics to show us how families were always worse off when they received support directly in the form of goods such as food than they would be if they received the equivalent amount of money. People who have money, he reminded us, have the opportunity to spend that money however they think best, and people always know better than bureaucrats or charities what their families need most. The greatest gift of income security, though, is the ability to take risks and to imagine different outcomes. If Mincome was successful, it would create income security for many more families, and allow young people in particular to imagine different kinds of lives than their parents lived.

I decided to change my major to economics.

The Basic Income Experiments

Forty years ago, basic income field experiments were taking place all across North America.[1] In the United States, they were called negative income tax experiments, while in Canada they were referred to as experiments in guaranteed annual income. In the 1970s, basic income was heralded as an end to poverty. In the United States, the civil rights movement of the 1960s had exposed many middle-class Americans for the first time to the existence of extreme poverty in what was otherwise a wealthy country. Young, idealistic students travelled from New York and Boston and New Haven to southern states to help with voter registration and were shocked to see Americans living in conditions they associated with low-income countries. The experiments were one response. In Canada, Mincome was constructed in the same atmosphere of possibility and expansion that led us to introduce the Canada Pension Plan in 1966 and nationwide universal health insurance by 1972, and to make unemployment insurance and disability support payments more generous. The world was being remade and, in Canada, what was then called guaranteed annual income was perceived to be one pillar of a just society — just like medicare.[2]

Mincome took place in three sites in Manitoba — Winnipeg, Dauphin and a set of smaller rural communities. The small town of Dauphin, an agriculturally dependent town in central Manitoba with about ten thousand residents, was unique because it was the only site in any of these experiments that was designated a saturation site: every family (rather than a selected few) that lived in the town was invited to participate. They would receive cash payments only if their family income was low enough to qualify. The amount of money they received would depend on the size of their family and the amount of income they received from other sources. The payments were modest: for a family of four with no other income, the basic income would be $3,800 (just over $22,000 in today's dollars). As income from other sources increased, the value of the basic income would decline by fifty cents for every dollar earned. A family of four earning $7,600 or more would receive nothing.

For people who had previously been receiving income assistance, these rates were only very slightly more generous. Their material circumstances would not be greatly affected. They would, however, have the freedom to spend their time and their money as they saw fit. If they wanted to attend school, they did not need the permission of a caseworker. If they wanted to open a business, they could do so. As long as their income was low enough to qualify, they received support. Perhaps because they were not treated with suspicion by caseworkers, families did not perceive their Mincome stipend as welfare and reported that they felt no stigma.[3] The people for whom Mincome made a profound financial difference were working people. As in many small towns, Dauphin had a number of seasonal, low-paid jobs, and many people were self-employed. They suffered a great deal of income insecurity because of the nature of agricultural work, and their earned incomes were often low enough that they qualified for partial stipends from Mincome even when they worked. The standard of living and economic security of the working poor in Dauphin expanded dramatically during Mincome.

The Death and Rediscovery of Mincome

The money flowed into Dauphin for only three years between 1975 and 1978, as planned. I completed my degree in economics and went on to graduate school, where economics had more to do with mathematics than with the living conditions of the poor. I lost track of Mincome. In fact, I was not alone. The 1970s were a turbulent time, both politically and economically. Oil prices increased as oil-producing countries in the Middle East recognized their newfound power. In Canada, high unemployment and inflation were running hand in hand, which seemed to contradict the way economists expected the world to work. Inflation exceeded 10 per cent a year, and many seniors suffered as the value of their savings evaporated. Young people buying houses faced interest rates of 18 per cent. Governments borrowed and spent money to stimulate the economy and create jobs, facing opposition over growing deficits and government debt. Workers went on strike, demanding cost of living increases. The 1970s began in idealism, and there was a clear focus on reducing poverty; by 1978, battered governments were trying to shore up the economy on many fronts. Poverty took a back seat. In the United States, the same economic challenges were compounded by political challenges as the experiments lost support in the House of Representatives and in the Senate.

Governments in Canada paid a price for economic upheaval. The social-democratic NDP government in Manitoba fell in 1976 and was replaced by a Progressive Conservative government. Few governments are keen to invest in the special projects of their predecessors. The Liberals in office federally were a minority government with most of their attention focused on survival. Mincome was cost-shared, with the federal government paying 75 per cent of the costs, and the province paying 25 per cent. As Mincome payments drew to an end, the researchers conducting the experiment petitioned the funders for more money to complete the analysis. They were refused and ordered to "archive the data for future analysis." The experiment ended with data in 1,800 cardboard boxes in a rented office suite in downtown Winnipeg, and at least two levels of government bickering about who should pay the rent.

The stated purpose of all the basic income experiments was to determine the impact on the labour market: would people work less if they were offered a basic income? Several years after the project ended, Derek Hum (the second research director of Mincome) and Wayne Simpson (a labour economist at the University of Manitoba) attempted to answer that question. They examined the Winnipeg sample and discovered that for adult men and single women, there was little effect. Two groups of people, however, reduced their work effort significantly. Married women, who were entitled to only four unpaid weeks of maternity leave at the time, chose to use the Mincome stipend to buy themselves longer maternity leaves. And young, unattached males reduced their work effort substantially.[4] But policy attention had shifted, and the results of Mincome were not at the top of anyone's mind. These young, unattached males, however, held an important clue that I would later investigate.

In the meantime, I finished my PhD and was hired as a professor of economics at the University of Manitoba. By 2000, I was working in the medical school, and every project I was involved with highlighted the intimate relationship between income and health outcomes. The disparities are profound: lower incomes are associated with shorter life expectancies, higher rates of self-harm and higher rates of chronic conditions. Having become ill, low-income individuals are more likely to suffer complications from their conditions. Even universal health care did not guarantee equal health outcomes for everyone. These statistical findings became real when I walked through the Health Sciences Centre in Winnipeg that treated many low-income residents of the surrounding neighbourhood as well as people flown in from northern communities for treatment. I talked to patients in the cafeteria, the hallways and the garden and soon came to understand a little better how the many different aspects of deprivation build on one another to undermine health. I could see, but still couldn't really understand, how a thirty-five-year-old could lose a leg to diabetes, or a teenager could be diagnosed with tuberculosis. It was clear enough that poverty was associated with poor health outcomes, but I wondered whether reducing the poverty in which people lived would actually improve their health. Then I remembered Mincome.

I went in search of the Mincome data. The data tape that Derek Hum and Wayne Simpson had used for their labour market analysis had become obsolete and, in any case, focused only on the Winnipeg sample. However, I knew the boxes were somewhere. I tracked them down to a regional office of Library and Archives Canada, where I confronted the full visual impact of 1,800 cubic feet of data.

Overwhelming as the data was, my graduate students and I began combing through the boxes and contemplating different ways of uncovering the impact of Mincome on health. The boxes contained not only the regular labour-market surveys that had informed Derek Hum and Wayne Simpson's work on labour markets, but all kinds of short surveys, letters from participants, information booklets, newspaper articles and the kind of ephemera that gives historians a sense of the period. We began to work through the boxes, and news of our work spread. Former participants phoned and emailed to tell me stories about the impact Mincome had had on their lives. Some of the participants who reflected on their experiences after three decades reported that the extra money had made life just a little bit easier. Mincome had allowed families living close to the edge to indulge in the small, everyday luxuries that make life tolerable. It reduced the stress of unexpected expenses. People reported that accepting the money did not make them feel bad because "everyone was the same." Others told stories of being able to make decisions with long-term consequences. One single mother with two young daughters reported that she had left welfare to join Mincome because she would have the freedom to take some job training, which her otherwise supportive welfare caseworker couldn't see the point of. Forty years later, she reflected on the pride she felt in having modelled independence for her daughters. A farm family that sold vegetables at a local market had faced hardship when their farm truck had broken down; Mincome had allowed them to buy a new truck and stay in business. Another woman told the story of how she and her husband, both in their early twenties at the time, had opened a small shop, relying on Mincome to pay their living expenses during the challenging early years of the business.

All the stories, whether they were about the small businesses that participants had started or been able to keep alive, or about children going off to college, or even adults able to take job training and make better decisions for their families, confirmed what I had been taught in my first year of university: families know better than any bureaucrat what they need. And what poor people undeniably need is money. Money gives people choices and opportunities.

Education and Mincome

My project, however, was focused on health and well-being. The Mincome money had flowed for only three years, and I was confronted with a limited budget and 1,800 boxes. Would the experiment have lasted long enough to affect people's lives? And would I be able to show the impact? I knew that I would require funding to complete the research, and that granting agencies would be skeptical that such old material could yield anything of interest. I thought again about the "young, unattached males" that reduced the number of hours they worked when Mincome was introduced. Translating social science into English, I knew that we were talking about adolescent boys — young men the same age I was in 1973, when I decided to complete grade thirteen rather than quit school to take a job as a bank teller or telephone operator.

When I quizzed some of the Mincome participants about their lives, several people from Dauphin explained that before Mincome was available, their older brothers and cousins had been under a significant amount of family pressure to become self-supporting as soon as possible, so that families could concentrate their financial resources on younger children. No one quite saw the point of staying in school when you could work and earn decent money. When Mincome came along, many of these families decided that they could support their adolescent sons a bit longer. Whether these boys went back to school because they aspired to a larger lifetime income, or just because they wanted to play football for another year, it would have a significant impact on their future lives. But how could we find these results in the data?

I called the provincial Department of Education and asked for enrollment data for all Manitoba high schools. I wondered whether the impact of Mincome would be large enough to show up in such aggregate data. I divided the data into Dauphin high schools, Winnipeg high schools and high schools in the rest of Manitoba. To get a crude measurement of high school completion rates, I divided grade twelve enrollments by the previous year's grade eleven enrollments:

Figure 2.1   Grade 12 Enrollment as Per cent of Previous Year Grade 11 Enrollment

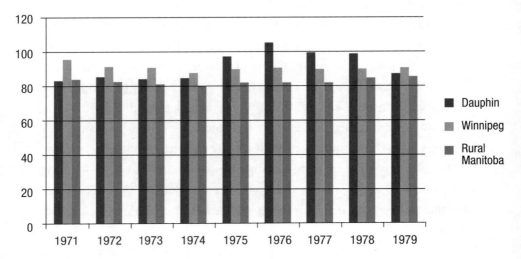

Source: Evelyn L. Forget, "The Town With No Poverty," *Canadian Public Policy* 37, no. 3 (2011).

If everyone in grade eleven continues to grade twelve, and there is no change in the underlying population, the bar in Figure 2.1 will reach 100. The larger the dropout rates between grade eleven and grade twelve, when most children are old enough to leave school legally, the lower the bar. Before 1975, there is little difference between Dauphin and the rest of rural Manitoba. As we might expect, adolescents living in Winnipeg were more likely to go on to grade twelve. When Mincome was introduced, the continuation rate in Dauphin increased above even the Winnipeg rate. In 1976, the bar exceeded 100 per cent; students who had left school were returning to complete grade twelve. In 1977 and 1978, the Dauphin continuation rate hovered near 100 per cent. When Mincome ended in 1979, Dauphin continuation rates fell back to the level of the rest of rural Manitoba. Mincome allowed a lucky cohort of "young, unattached males" to aspire to a much better life than they might have expected had they left school to work like their older brothers and cousins. The decline in hours worked documented by Derek Hum and Wayne Simpson, which on the surface seems to support the fear that basic income will encourage laziness, is actually a good news story.

Imagine the life chances experienced by someone who did not finish high school in the mid-1970s. Young men had access to good jobs. In Dauphin, they left school to take relatively well-paying jobs in agriculture, agriculture-servicing industries and manufacturing. Since the 1970s, the number of people employed in agriculture has fallen dramatically, and factories have closed in the face of increased international competition and, especially, automation. These young men who left school early found jobs that would soon be undermined by a changing economy. Without a high school diploma, they would have struggled to find and keep work as time passed. High school graduates are much less likely to experience periods of unemployment than those without a diploma, and when they are laid off they are more likely to be re-employed at wages comparable to those of the jobs they left behind. Their lifetime earnings are higher and the opportunities they can offer their children greater.

Mincome and Health Outcomes

My project, though, was especially concerned with health outcomes. Did reducing poverty make people healthier? Mincome was not designed to gather health data; its purpose was to address the fear that families who were offered a basic income would reduce the number of hours they worked for wages. I was able to find the health outcomes only because of a set of lucky accidents. By 1972, all provinces in Canada had introduced universal health insurance. One of the features of Canadian medicare is that it routinely collects a great deal of data as we use the health care system. Every time an individual interacts with hospitals or physicians, a record of that interaction is created. Hospitalizations are recorded in a database along with records of the patient including, most significantly, how long they were hospitalized, what happened to them in the hospital, and why they were hospital-ized in the first place. Every time someone goes to a family doctor, the doctor completes a billing claim for the province. The billing claim identifies the patient, the date and the reason for the consultation.[5] As you might imagine, this is highly confidential data, and great care is taken to protect the privacy of Canadians.

Over time, these data in Manitoba have been de-identified — that is, patient names and identifying characteristics have been removed — and made available to qualified researchers under very restricted conditions. Consequently, the database contains everyone who lived in Dauphin during the Mincome experiment. It was also possible to find people of the same age and sex who lived in similar kinds of families and similar towns. Therefore, we could create a set of matched con-trols — three other people of the same age, sex, family type and living arrangements — for every person who lived in Dauphin. By examining how these controls fared and comparing their results to the Dauphin residents, we found that:

- Hospitalizations for Dauphin residents fell 8.5 per cent relative to the controls;

- "Accidents and injuries" and "mental health" accounted for most of the decline;

- Visits to family doctors by Dauphin residents fell relative to the controls;

- "Mental health" issues accounted for most of the decline in visits to family doctors.

"Accidents and injuries" is a very big category that includes such things as car and workplace accidents, self-harm and accidental poisoning, assaults and family violence and so on. Low income and "accident and injury" hospitalizations are often linked, partly because low-income

people tend to work at more dangerous jobs and live in more dangerous housing and neighbourhoods. The link between mental health and
low income also seems reasonable; the constant stress of money worries can lead to anxiety and depression. Health did seem to improve for
Dauphin residents, relative to the controls, during Mincome. Mental
health improvements were especially important.

How Did Mincome Make People Healthier?

The statistical analysis of Mincome participants showed undeniably
that people used fewer health services when they had a basic income
available to them. They were hospitalized less frequently and visited
family doctors less often. We also know that improved mental health
seemed to play a key role. Statistical analysis, however, cannot explain
how or why something happened. What was the mechanism through
which health improved? For that, we need the memories of participants.

Without question, Mincome reduced material deprivation. Mincome
rates in Dauphin were set at a level just slightly more generous than
income assistance. The monetary benefit for income assistance recipients who switched to Mincome was minimal. However, Mincome also
offered stipends to low-income working people who had previously not
had access to such benefits. These working people, who outnumbered
income assistance recipients, did see their income increase.

Eric Richardson, who was about twelve when his family participated
in Mincome, has a vivid memory of going to the dentist for the first
time: "They didn't take you to the dentist unless you were in pain. No
one had extra money for that. I remember being lined up with my
brother and sister and marched off to the dentist about then. I ended
up with a mouthful of fillings. So — thanks, Mincome!"

Mincome meant money was available for non-emergency care that
could lead to better health, even if the benefits eluded a twelve-year-old.
There is, however, reason to believe more was going on.

More important than the money received by Mincome recipients was the insurance aspect of basic income. Everyone in Dauphin

received the promise that they could receive income support if their income fell below the program threshold. This had the effect of dramatically reducing income insecurity in a town in which much employment and employment income was dependent on agriculture, either directly or indirectly. A bad year for canola reduced the income of the farmer, but it also reduced the incomes of farm labourers, truck drivers, used car salesmen, hairdressers, restaurant owners, small shopkeepers and almost everyone else in town. If this was the nature of small-town employment forty years ago, it is increasingly coming to characterize much larger segments of the labour market today. Precarious employment is growing as a proportion of all employment in Canada and is strongly associated with worse employee health.[6]

Even people who never actually collected a stipend from Mincome knew that the program existed and benefited from it as a form of insurance, particularly those near to the qualifying threshold. Many people didn't know in advance whether they would qualify for Mincome support; it would depend on the weather and other unpredictable events. One question asked of Mincome recipients by the research team was "Why did you choose to participate in Mincome?" The most frequently cited response was "because it would be there if I needed it."[7] Just as in the case of fire or car insurance, a basic income benefits even those who do not need to collect. Anxiety is reduced simply because the insurance exists.

Mincome was also associated with a strong feeling of community in Dauphin. The program did not materially affect the degree of income inequality, largely because even the highest incomes in Dauphin — those of physicians or high school principals — were not nearly as far removed from the incomes of ordinary workers as those of high-income earners in large urban centres are today. The poorest residents were a little less deprived under the program. However, the way that Mincome affected life in this small town reflected the kind of social cohesion often associated with better community health.

I remember those years as really good years. There was just
a little bit of money around. We started a small shop — we
sold record players and records — and people were always out
on the streets. Everyone had enough extra money to go out
for a beer after work. People socialized a lot. The shop never
actually paid us a salary. It paid its way, but Mincome helped
us a lot. When Mincome ended, things just got hard again. We
closed a year or so after Mincome — 1980, I think. — Lois

The marked increase in high school completion rates reflects these
social effects as well. Imagine how a seventeen-year-old decides whether
to go back to school to complete grade twelve or to leave and take a job.
He and his parents will consider the income available to the family, and
whether they can afford to support another year of school. If the family
expects to receive support from Mincome should they need it, parents
might encourage children to stay in school. The young man in question
will consider how the money he might earn would affect his life, but
he will also consider the attractions of continuing his education. One
of those attractions will be what his friends decide to do. If more of his
friends go back to school, he is more likely to consider the option. It
matters whether his friends are in families that might also benefit from
a basic income. The more families that participate, the more likely it
will be that boys continue to grade twelve. Even young men in families who do not receive support from Mincome will be influenced by
the decisions that their friends make. That is, the social attitudes that
govern community life will be influenced by a basic income.

This sense of community solidarity was also reflected in many of the
comments made by participants with whom I spoke:

"We were all in it together."

"Everyone was the same, so there was no shame."

"We all helped each other out. When we got the truck, we were always
hauling for people. Dad had the best truck, so if someone had some
lambs to ship, they used our truck."

It is possible that Mincome was associated with social solidarity because the town itself worked that way whether or not people received support through Mincome. None of the other experiments in North America during the 1970s had a saturation site where everyone in town had a similar offer. Normally, these experiments are conducted as randomized controlled trials, as was the case in the Winnipeg site. A randomized controlled trial means that the researchers came to town and selected a fairly small proportion of the total population to participate. These participants were then put into either the treatment group that received support through Mincome, or a control group that did not. The idea was that if you compared the results of the two groups, any differences would be due to the existence of Mincome. The participants in the experiment in a randomized controlled trial would know each other only by accident. Therefore, you would not see the kind of social effects that people remember so fondly from the Dauphin site.

There have been other experiments, mostly in low- and middle-income countries such as Kenya and India, in which entire villages are treated (as was the case with Dauphin). In almost all cases, researchers documented similar kinds of social outcomes. In Malawi, social attitudes about early marriages and transactional sex work were affected by a basic income, and the lives of young girls improved as a consequence.[8] In India, social transformation was at the heart of findings.[9] Similar kinds of findings emerge in almost all kinds of similarly designed projects. When everyone is eligible to receive a basic income, whether the stipend depends on income or is received by everyone, social attitudes tend to change. In low-income countries, development goals such as female education are met; in middle-income countries, children are less likely to work at menial tasks[10] while women are empowered to make independent decisions about their lives and work efforts.[11]

This sense of social support is one of the most significant determinants of population health although it manifests itself in distinct ways depending on social context. Basic income has been found to support social solidarity in various places around the world. One of the great outstanding questions awaiting the results of the new round of experiments underway as of 2018 is whether and to what extent a basic income will enhance social solidarity in an urban setting in high-income countries. We are not likely to revert to the intimate life of a prairie town in the 1970s any more than we are likely to revert to the labour market of the 1950s. However, the very idea of a basic income, whether it is targeted or universally available, depends on the recognition that we are interdependent, and we all benefit from a basic income in the form of a more stable, prosperous and inclusive society, whether or not we receive a stipend.

Chapter 3

Basic Income is Good for Your Health

As Canadians, we often take pride in our universal health care system, and we think it means everyone has access to medically necessary care, notwithstanding perennial concerns about wait times that do not seem to be much worse for low-income than for high-income Canadians. If we think about it a bit more, we realize that many health services are not paid for by the government but require individual insurance or out-of-pocket payments: dental care and prescription medications are most pressing. However, almost all income assistance programs offer recipients extended health benefits that include dental care and prescriptions. In some provinces, children and seniors receive these services without a means test. If access to health services is the primary determinant of how healthy we are, then our health should not depend on our incomes.

And yet our hospitals are full of people who are there not because they have bad luck or faulty genes, but because they have spent years living in deteriorating housing, working badly paid and physically demanding jobs, eating inadequate diets and living with economic insecurity and the stigma associated with poverty. Their bodies are not injured as much as worn out; chronic conditions such as diabetes, hypertension, arthritis and cardiovascular disease have replaced infectious diseases as the primary causes of hospitalization and death, and chronic conditions even more than infectious diseases are strongly influenced by the broader circumstances of our lives.[1] Stress associated with economic insecurity encourages behaviours such as smoking and alcohol and drug consumption, which worsen health conditions. In the poorest neighbourhoods in Canada, men die on average a full four years before their counterparts who live in the wealthiest neighbourhoods. For women, the difference is two years.[2] In Winnipeg, the numbers are even more startling: in East St. Paul, the neighbourhood with the highest median income, women lived on average to 87.5 years in 2011, and men lived until 82.3, but in the income-challenged North End, women only lived to be 70.9 years old, and men died on average at 66.7. That means a woman in the wealthiest neighbourhood of Winnipeg outlived her counterpart in the poorest neighbourhood by 16.6 years, while a man living in the wealthiest neighbourhood lived 15.6 years longer than a man in the poorest neighbourhood. And that gap is growing. Five years earlier, the life-expectancy gap for men was 13.4 years.[3] Stroke and heart attack rates show similar patterns, and rates of dementia are almost twice as high for the poorest as for the richest, even when we adjust for age and sex.

At every stage of our lives, our health is affected by our biological and genetic inheritance, our physical environment, our behaviour, our access to health services and the social and economic factors that surround us. Children in poor families are more likely to be born too early and too small, which affects their health and education throughout childhood. Mothers who suffer stress during pregnancy can bear children with a higher risk of developing diabetes. Young mothers who are depressed have children with higher rates of educational difficulties and poorer health outcomes. Children raised in poverty are less likely to live in safe neighbourhoods and safe housing and more likely to suffer accidents and injuries. Rates of asthma are higher for poor children, and educational attainment is lower. They are more likely to be behind in school and to score poorly on standardized tests. Children from the poorest families change schools more often and come to the attention of Child and Family Services more frequently.[4] As they get older, they are more likely to give birth as adolescents (early births are associated with poorer outcomes for children and parents) and to be diagnosed with sexually transmitted infections. Children raised in poverty are, as adults, more likely to experience addictions, mental health difficulties, physical disabilities and premature death (defined as any death before age seventy-five). They are also less likely to graduate from high school on time, and more likely to live in poverty as adults. Poor adults are diagnosed with chronic diseases at younger ages and suffer more complications. They have more accidents throughout their lives and are more likely to suffer dementia before their too-early deaths.[5] Even people who eventually escape from poverty must deal with the consequences of the health conditions they acquired earlier in life.

In work conducted for the World Health Organization, Sir Michael Marmot identifies the social determinants of health as "the conditions in which people are born, grow, live, work and age. The conditions are shaped by the distribution of money, power and resources at local, national and global levels — sometimes termed structural determinants of health inequalities."[6] While health services and biology are important, they are not as important as the social and physical surroundings in which we live. The Public Health Agency of Canada lists twelve key determinants of health[7]:

1. Income and Social Status

2. Social Support Networks

3. Education and Literacy

4. Employment/Working Conditions

5. Social Environments

6. Physical Environments

7. Personal Health Practices and Coping Skills

8. Healthy Child Development

9. Biology and Genetic Endowment

10. Health Services

11. Gender

12. Culture

This list is not definitive. Dennis Raphael lists fourteen closely related determinants of the health of Canadians: aboriginal status, disability status, gender, early life, income and income distribution, education, race, employment and working conditions, social exclusion, food insecurity, housing, social safety net, health services, unemployment and job security.[8] However we define them, the social and physical conditions in which we live have a strong impact on how healthy we are at every stage of our lives.

These factors interact with one another in complex ways. For example, education influences the kind of job you work at and the level of income you earn. It affects how likely you are to be unemployed. Income earned determines the kind of housing you have and the neighbourhood you live in. The level of education you attain can affect your coping skills, but your coping skills also influence the level of education you are likely to achieve. Gender, race and culture influence your income and your job prospects. Health is determined by individual lifestyle factors, social and community networks and the general socioeconomic, cultural and environmental conditions in which individuals and families live.[9]

Over the past five decades, the evidence linking our social and physical environments to our health has become overwhelming. Most of the statistical evidence we have collected shows a correlation between income and health for a wide variety of health outcomes: premature death, rates of chronic and infectious diseases, rates of disability, complication rates after surgery, and various health indices. This association is true not only for the poorest among us; at every income level, people with higher incomes are healthier than people with slightly less income. This has led to a set of theories attempting to explain how health and income are linked.

How do we know for sure that poor health is caused by low incomes and not the other way around? Perhaps low incomes and poor health are correlated because sick people are less likely to work, take more time off work when they are employed and are unable to work at peak efficiency even when they do work. It certainly is the case that people with health conditions and disabilities suffer challenges in the job market and usually earn less than healthy people and people without disabilities. However, income is strongly related to birth outcomes and child health outcomes, and children are not normally expected to be working. Other studies look at when income changes and when health changes; they note that income is more likely to decline before health declines and not the other way around. The evidence that low income causes poor health is overwhelming. The fundamental role played by income is so profound that income is sometimes referred to as the determinant of determinants. There are several pathways through which low income is believed to cause poor health, some of which affect the individual and some of which influence outcomes through their impact on the organization of society.

Material Deprivation

The most basic effect of income is through material deprivation. Families with low incomes cannot easily afford to buy nutritious food or to live in decent housing in safe neighbourhoods. One indicator of material deprivation identifies those families who struggle to put food on the table. Scholars such as Valerie Tarasuk use food insecurity as a measure of extreme deprivation. Tarasuk has shown that low income is the best predictor of food insecurity. Lynn McIntyre has shown that food insecurity declines markedly as soon as a low-income individual turns sixty-five, largely because their income from Old Age Security and the Guaranteed Income Supplement is much greater than it was under provincial income assistance. Low-income families have difficulty accessing health care that is not provided without charge. Low-waged workers without a drug plan at work may scrimp on prescription drugs. Their oral health will suffer if they cannot pay a dentist through workplace benefits. They might not visit clinics for routine or follow-up visits if public transport is not readily available. All these health-related decisions and many others will be compromised by inadequate incomes.[10]

However, if material deprivation alone were the cause of poor health outcomes, we would expect to see the health disparities related to income disappear once incomes reach a fairly moderate level. Middle-income Canadians can afford dental care, most prescription drugs, decent diets and housing and reasonable transportation. Why would the disparity persist as incomes increase even more? One suggestion is that income affects health through the experience of chronic stress.

Chronic stress has been linked to a variety of hormonal and neurological changes that result in poor health. It impairs memory and increases the risk of depression, lowers immune response, elevates blood pressure and the risk of cardiovascular disease and affects hormonal systems. People who are already vulnerable are especially liable to experience poorer mental health and cognitive outcomes. Chronic stress sometimes leads to negative coping behaviours, such as smoking, alcohol abuse and other addictions. That is, chronic stress may account for much of the variance in health and social outcomes associated with the harmful aspects of lower social status.[11]

Unlike material deprivation, which might be expected to disappear as income increases, chronic stress exists along a continuum. One particular factor associated with chronic stress is economic insecurity, which can affect individuals at any income level. A young mother who relies on provincial income assistance suffers from income insecurity, but so do low-income workers facing economic insecurity because they have no idea how many hours they might be able to work or whether their contract will be renewed, as well as entrepreneurs whose income insecurity is related to market conditions beyond their control.

Economic Insecurity

Economic insecurity is not the same thing as low income. People with very low, but stable and predictable, defined-benefit pensions do not suffer from economic insecurity. They may suffer from low income and, sometimes, material deprivation. By contrast, people with moderate incomes live with income insecurity if their jobs and incomes are subject to sudden and unpredictable changes. Economic insecurity exists when a family fears that its income might fall dramatically without advance notice and without the resources necessary to ride out the risk. Economic insecurity is a state of mind rather than a characteristic of an income flow. It can be offset by insurance, such as Employment Insurance, or by sufficient savings to deal with unexpected shortfalls. Economic insecurity can persist even when income is stable if people fear changes in their economic situation. Someone who works on a short-term contract might earn a relatively high income, but if the contract itself is subject to cancellation, and there is no insurance or wealth to fill the gaps between contracts, then that individual would suffer from income insecurity. Job insecurity is the greatest cause of income insecurity but not the only cause.

There is a deep literature on the causes and consequences of job insecurity. The new economy has been revealing itself for many years, but since the 2008 financial crisis, it has become increasingly impossible to ignore the growing numbers of workers who spend many years or their entire careers working on insecure, short-term contracts. All of this contributes to chronic stress, which itself leads to poorer health.

Economic Inequality

Within any given country, some people do much better than others. Richard Wilkinson and Kate Pickett argued in *The Spirit Level* that there is a strong causal relationship between inequality and a wide variety of population health outcomes observed in different settings over a number of years. More equal societies do better than less equal societies. Violent crime rates are lower, and people live longer. Very early births are less common, and children are more likely to finish high school on time. Prevalence of chronic disease is lower, and when people do get ill, they are less likely to suffer secondary effects that reduce the quality of their lives. Not only do people live longer, but they spend more years in good health. Children also have better health in more equal societies and do better in school.[12]

Income inequality, like income insecurity, might also affect health outcomes through increases in chronic stress. Large income differences between rich and poor seem to worsen most of the problems associated with low income. Health outcomes that are strongly related to social status, such as poor birth outcomes, are particularly vulnerable to rising income inequality. It may be that inequality leads people to constantly compare their aspirations and achievements with others', and to suffer stress when they fall short.

However, income inequality has an effect that goes beyond the individual. Income inequality is a collective measure; it measures how equally a society's resources are shared, and when these resources are shared more equally, everyone is better off. In more unequal US states, people score lower on "agreeableness," which measures how concerned they are about getting along with others. In more unequal European countries, people show less solidarity and less willingness to help others. More equal societies may be healthier because they are more cohesive and enjoy better social relations, both of which are associated with better population health.[13]

Since the 2008 financial crisis, people have become very concerned about inequality, but it is easy to be confused about what is actually happening. Income inequality is growing not because the poor are getting poorer, but because a few Canadians are doing exceptionally well. The income growth of the top 5 per cent of earners is much larger than that of the top 10 per cent, and that of the top 1 per cent dramatically larger than that of the top 5 per cent. However, inequality overall in Canada has been growing relatively modestly since 2008, unlike in the United States and some European countries. Much of the existing income inequality in this country occurred before the 2008 recession. Since the 1970s, there has been a general stagnation in wage income, particularly for those with high school education or less. While the economy grew and created economic opportunity for investors and for highly skilled labour, not everyone shared the gains equally.

What really worries us is a growing gap in aspirations and lifestyles between those who graduated from high school and completed some higher education, and those with a high school education or less. This perceived gap is fed by the greater role played by social media in our lives. The feeling of being left behind is enhanced by the flood of achievements and possessions posted by others, and the sheer speed at which perceptions occur in this realm does not encourage critical appraisal. Even old-fashioned media has been overwhelmed by reality TV that encourages interpersonal comparisons. This focus on personal achievement and personal possessions creates the impression that everyone else is doing better than we are and living happier and more productive lives. This perception of growing social disparities may be less real than perceived, but it still causes chronic stress among those struggling to keep up. It also fractures the sense of solidarity that is essential to social well-being.

A Decline in Social Solidarity

Our growing unease in Canada is also heightened by observed changes in the United States. Not only is the growth of income inequality much stronger in the United States than elsewhere in the industrial world, but the manifestation of inequality in terms of social divisions is also starker. This decline in social solidarity affects population health in dramatic ways. Richard Reeves argues that the essential divide in US society is not the perceived gap between the top 1 per cent (or even 0.01

per cent), who benefit from economic change, and the rest of society facing stagnant incomes, but rather the gap between the top 20 per cent — the upper middle class — and the rest of society. The growing separation is apparent in where people live, how they form families, their lifestyles and, especially, their attitudes. Reeves argues that members of the upper middle class are becoming more effective at passing their status along to their children through the use of zoning laws that encourage homogeneous neighbourhoods and schools, college application processes and the allocation of internships. This reduces overall social mobility and hardens attitudes among the privileged against efforts to enhance equality and broaden opportunities. These entrenched attitudes mean that political efforts to reduce the gap will be met by vocal opposition.[14]

The decline of social solidarity is especially associated with a variety of negative mental health outcomes. In 2017, the *World Happiness Report* published the results of a series of surveys designed to measure how people in countries all around the world felt about their lives. One of the most surprising results was the sudden and steep decline in American well-being. Between 2006 and 2016, the United States fell from number three (of thirty-three countries) to number nineteen (of thirty-four countries).[15] This was not the result of a declining economy or even declining physical health outcomes. On average, the United States did well economically, but the gains were not equally distributed across the population, and this disparity is reflected in the other four factors that measure social solidarity.[16] The United States lost ground on four significant factors: social support; perceived corruption of business and government; freedom to make life choices; and generosity of donations. Social well-being cannot be improved through economic growth alone. If the US scores were returned to their 2006 levels for these four factors, well-being would increase dramatically. To achieve the same increase in well-being through economic growth alone, GDP per capita would have to increase from $53,000 to $133,000.

The decline in social well-being in the United States shows up in various ways. Economists Anne Case and Angus Deaton have spent a lot of time in the past decade investigating the US malaise, and they make an even bolder claim. Other studies largely corroborate their results while challenging some of the details.[17] Case and Deaton identify a series of deaths that they label "deaths of despair" — that is, death by suicide, drug poisoning and alcohol — that they believe increase as social well-being declines. They document an increase in the death rate associated with these causes over the past two decades among white fifty- to fifty-four-year-olds with a high school diploma or less, and argue that growing economic disparities are responsible. Case and Deaton suggest that it is the "crushed aspirations" of poorly educated, white workers struggling to find and keep jobs in a changing economy that have led them to replace stable marriages with serial monogamy, to drop out of the workforce and to replace their participation in traditional communal churches with attendance at "prosperity gospel churches" that emphasize individual identity. Low-income minorities have fared even worse in absolute terms but there is no similar increase in the death rate associated with these causes, possibly because their expectations were more modest to begin with. While white workers watched and despaired as jobs they considered their birthright disappeared, other workers have always been more skeptical that the American Dream was within reach. These are all aspects of an unhealthy, and increasingly unequal, society.

Case and Deaton found similar but not nearly so dramatic results in other countries that have faced similar economic challenges in recent years. In Canada, for example, the death rate due to drugs, alcohol and suicide among this age group is increasing, but very modestly. Case and Deaton attribute these different international experiences to the fact that most of the other countries they investigated still have reasonably functional social safety nets, including at least basic welfare and social medicine, unlike the social welfare system in the United States.

I am struck by the realization that Case and Deaton's despairing fifty- to fifty-four-year-olds are exactly the same age as the many young men from Dauphin who were permitted, by Mincome, to finish high school. Even though Case and Deaton did not find the same stark empirical evidence for Canada that they found in the United States, there is no doubt that young men who were encouraged by family poverty to leave school early struggled in their later lives as compared to their lucky contemporaries who had different opportunities because they finished high school.

It is easy to focus on the health consequences of income inequality because income is relatively easy to measure, but the divisions in society go beyond mere income. As Reeves and others have suggested in the US case, it may be the decline of social solidarity that leads to the mental health outcomes that Anne Case and Angus Deaton capture in their deaths of despair. Social solidarity is threatened by growing income inequality, but it also worsened by gaps in education and opportunity that extend far deeper than income.

Basic income alone will not and cannot eliminate the growing income inequality that seems to be a feature of the changing economy. Basic income provides resources at the bottom end of the income distribution; it allows people who haven't accumulated resources of their own to withstand unexpected events, such as a sudden job loss or an illness or accident, and to develop the resilience necessary to recover and to reclaim their previous lifestyle. High incomes, however, have been increasing much more quickly than average incomes and, over time, more and more resources are being accumulated by smaller numbers of people who are lucky enough to possess the necessary skills to benefit from the changing economy.

Basic Income Can Help

Basic income alone cannot eliminate all the growing divisions in society. It can, however, address such fundamental issues as material deprivation and income insecurity. A basic income is designed precisely to reduce the debilitating chronic stress associated with these factors. Moreover, a basic income may address some of the social exclusion associated with poverty. People with the resources to allow their children to participate in low-paid internships or to attend university can give their children a fair chance to benefit from opportunities that high-income families take for granted. All of these outcomes lead to better individual and population health.

There is a monetary return on these benefits to population health. We spend an inordinate amount of money in this country on the provision of health care. Hospital care alone costs more than sixty billion dollars every year. As we saw in the Mincome experiment, basic income recipients are less likely to need to be hospitalized compared with similar individuals who do not receive a basic income. Does it not make sense to invest more money upfront in a basic income program that gives individuals and families the resources they need to live better, more fulfilling lives? That investment will pay off in a need for fewer hospital beds and lower demands placed on family doctors, who too often find themselves prescribing antidepressants and anti-anxiety medications to people living with the stress of chronic poverty and economic insecurity. Poverty and economic insecurity are extremely expensive, and nowhere are the costs more apparent than in our overburdened health care system. If we want to make health care sustainable in Canada — to get the costs of delivering health under control — then we need to do a better job of addressing the factors leading to poor health.

Chapter 4
The Future of Work

"There is a pretty good chance we end up with a universal basic income or something like that due to automation."
— Elon Musk[1]

"A lot of exciting new innovations are going to be created, which will generate a lot of opportunities and a lot of wealth, but there is a real danger it could also reduce the amount of jobs. This will make experimenting with ideas like basic income even more important in the years to come."
— Richard Branson[2]

"We should have a society that measures progress not just by economic metrics like GDP, but by how many of us have a role we find meaningful. We should explore ideas like universal basic income to make sure everyone has a cushion to try new ideas."
— Mark Zuckerberg, in a May 2017 Harvard commencement speech[3]

"If machines produce everything we need, the outcome will depend on how things are distributed. Everyone can enjoy a life of luxurious leisure if the machine-produced wealth is shared, or most people can end up miserably poor if the machine-owners successfully lobby against wealth redistribution. So far, the trend seems to be towards the second option, with technology driving ever-increasing inequality."

— Stephen Hawking[4]

When Mincome and the other experiments of the 1970s were designed, many critics worried that giving people money for nothing would discourage work. In all honesty, most taxpayers worried less about the psychological effect this might have on the workers than about its effect on the economy. Who would grow our food and drive the trucks and teach our kids and build our houses and make our cars? If fewer people worked, what would happen to the economic growth that supports our standard of living? Fewer people working, they reasoned, meant less for all of us.

One indication of how much the world has changed is that the justification for some of the current basic income experiments is a widely shared belief that, whether we want to or not, advances in robotics and artificial intelligence mean that many of us will be working less in the very near future. Silicon Valley entrepreneurs who invest in disruptive technologies and watch their incomes grow are often the first to sound the alarm: if machines can do the hard and dirty work of production — and do it faster, better and cheaper — then we don't need people to perform these tasks. To be sure, they recognize that human labour would still be necessary to program the machines and develop the new technologies (although advances in machine learning are calling even that into question), and probably to provide some kinds of work in hospitals, daycare centres and nursing homes (although advances in robotic technology are rapidly changing some kinds of surgery, and robots are providing companionship for frail seniors). However, the total number of person hours required to perform these tasks would be much smaller than we now employ in production. And the workers that would be required by this new economy are not the same people we are used to employing; miners can't be transformed into nursing home attendants overnight, and truck drivers do not easily become programmers. The problem, from the point of view of people like Elon Musk, is not how we can get people to work, but how we can get money into the hands of people who are not required to work. If we don't solve that problem, governments will be facing social unrest beyond anything they have witnessed so far. Displaced workers need to eat, and — at least as important from the perspective of people whose large incomes depend on these technologies — someone needs to buy all the new goods and services created by the machines. Basic income seems like an obvious solution.

The Old View of Productivity and Growth

Not everyone shares the sweeping visions emanating from California. Traditional policy advisors in the Bank of Canada, the Department of Finance and international agencies such as the Organisation for Economic Co-operation and Development (OECD) imagine the future unfolding much like the past. From their perspective, the problem we face today in Canada is just the opposite of the Silicon Valley prediction; they worry about an emerging labour shortage. All the goods and services we use in our daily lives, they point out, are the product of labour. All the social programs that support our children, the elderly and people with disabilities are paid for by taxes on people who work. Without workers, nothing would be produced. If we point to automation, they remind us that someone needs to create the robots, to program them, to oversee and repair them and to record the value of what they produce. If we talk about self-driving vehicles, they point to the massive investment of human effort that created such vehicles and the human ingenuity that will be required to repair them and to design the next technological breakthrough. Sure, factories now produce with smaller workforces because of automation, but there are so many more firms out there. Economic growth will create new jobs more quickly than automation will eliminate them.

We are reminded that an aging population means we must do everything possible to increase the proportion of the population working because fewer workers will have to pay the taxes that support the pensions and health care required by the massive baby boom cohort that is just beginning to retire. We must do everything in our power to increase the proportion of the population working: for example, offer daycare to keep parents of infants working and increase immigration so that a steady flow of younger immigrants can backfill the aging labour force. Not very long ago, the federal government attempted to increase the age of entitlement for Old Age Security from sixty-five to sixty-seven to encourage people to work for more years and to draw pensions for fewer years. According to these traditionalists, offering a basic income to people living in an economy on the brink of labour shortages is foolish; it will encourage people to work less when what we need desperately is for everyone to work more.

This story is based on enough fact that it seems credible. The Canadian population is certainly aging, but this generation of old people in high-income countries is among the richest and healthiest that has ever lived. The poverty rate among those over sixty-five is half that of younger people, and it is not only because of their government pensions. Canadians over sixty-five have benefited from the rapid expansion of the economy in the 1950s and 1960s, from the investment opportunities that saw modest savings expand and from the housing boom that created millionaires of ordinary workers. The fear that an aging workforce will place more demands for support on the smaller working-age populations to come is based on the assumptions that the aged are a net draw on social resources and that the only way to finance new programs is by imposing taxes on workers. Seniors do collect pensions and draw on health care, but they also pay income taxes on dividends and taxes on capital gains. The amassed wealth of seniors today is considerable, which lessens their reliance on Old Age Security and, especially, the Guaranteed Income Supplement. They are healthier than past generations and entering medically intensive personal care homes at lower rates.

There is something a little archaic about this story of looming disaster. It is based on the idea that the future will unfold just exactly like the past. To generate economic growth, this story claims, more and more people must work ever-longer hours for many more years. This depressing story of scarcity, unending toil and limited options flies in the face of the unbounded optimism of Silicon Valley, many of whose denizens regard it as unimaginative, backward-looking and more than a little mean-spirited.

Silicon Valley Utopianism

Y-Combinator, a venture capital accelerator that supports tech start-ups, has undertaken the task of developing a basic income experiment in two as-yet-unnamed US states. Sam Altman is its CEO. He argues that it will take somewhere between ten and one hundred years for advances in artificial intelligence to induce governments to start giving handouts to avoid mass riots. In a January 2016 blog post, he wrote, "Fifty years from now, I think it will seem ridiculous that we used fear of not being able to eat as a way to motivate people. I also think it's impossible to truly have equality of opportunity without some form of guaranteed income."[5]

These speculators argue that the first industrial revolution, which took place in the middle of the nineteenth century, relied on the steam engine and the creation of large factories. The second industrial revolution, early in the twentieth century, exploited the power of electricity and the internal combustion engine. The third automated production through electronics and information technology in the mid-twentieth century. The fourth, or digital, revolution has been underway since the middle of the last century. Billions of people linked by mobile devices with unprecedented access to knowledge and processing power, accompanied by disruptive technological changes in artificial intelligence, robotics, the internet of things, 3-D printing and nanotechnology, are remaking the world and the economy.

So far, the chief beneficiaries of this new economy have been consumers with enough income to access the digital world; we can stream music, play games, order a ride or dinner, work and watch a film in ways we couldn't imagine a few years ago. This world also holds the promise of more efficient production lines and lower-cost transportation and communication. Economic growth no longer means more people working at traditional jobs for more years, but fewer and fewer humans working to produce ever-larger quantities of the goods and services that we already consume and other commodities we can scarcely imagine.

If we can produce more and more with less labour, why encourage work? Jobs will be scarce and workers plentiful. We could all share existing jobs by working fewer hours or, alternatively, some people could continue to work while others withdraw from the workforce and occupy their time any way they like. They can draw pictures, take care of their aging parents or young children, write bad poetry (or literary masterpieces), volunteer, spend the summers canoeing and winters skiing or snuggle down in cafés inventing new apps and new games to occupy their fellow humans in our growing free time. The only challenge: who will buy the output created by the machines?

This story, as engaging as it is, is really too simple. Even though it sounds like something from science fiction, it is an old story that we've told ourselves many times throughout history: "rapid technological change is just over the horizon, and we are just on the edge of fifteen-hour work weeks and massive unemployment." Or, depending on the writer, "technological change is just about to transform society by freeing us from labour and giving us all time to become poets and philosophers." It is, in fact, a kind of zombie economics: an old idea that keeps struggling back to its feet no matter how many times history tries to kill it off.

Disruptive Technological Change Is Not New

This is not the first time in history that we have faced massive technological change. Some recent reports breathlessly forecast a future in which self-driving cars and trucks displace from the US workforce 1.6 million truck drivers, 800,000 delivery truck drivers, 180,000 taxi drivers, 160,000 Uber drivers, 500,000 school bus drivers and 160,000 transit bus drivers, not to mention the 445,000 auto body repair shop workers who will no longer be required to repair the consequences of higher accident rates associated with human driving error, the hospital workers no longer required to patch up human victims and the many associated jobs — in total, well over four million US jobs lost to just one foreseeable change.[6] In Canada, a study published by the Conference Board of Canada estimated that 560,000 people working in the transport, truck and courier service industries may lose work along with 50,000 taxi drivers and chauffeurs.[7]

What would a similar article written at the turn of the twentieth century have reported? Would we have heard that a massive new industry made feasible with lower-priced internal combustion engines would soon create millions of jobs worldwide not only for truck drivers, but in supporting industries, or would we have mourned for the horses, drivers, buggy manufacturers, farmers, train makers and engineers and others who would soon be displaced? In the nineteenth century, 80 per cent of Canadian jobs were in agriculture; today about 2 per cent of jobs are in agriculture, largely because of technological change that has substituted machinery for human labour. One tractor can do the work that previous generations relied on a dozen children to provide. Closer to our own time, do we focus on the new jobs in communications that computer software makes possible, or do we mourn the downturn in pulp and paper and the demise of local newspapers?

The original Luddites were nineteenth-century British weavers and textile workers who objected to the use of automatic looms and knitting frames in textile factories. The first computers were developed and implemented in nineteenth-century textile mills. Most of these workers had spent years learning their craft, and they feared (correctly) that the new equipment could be operated by unskilled operators who were robbing them of their livelihood. When their petitions to the government were ignored, some began breaking into the mills to destroy the machinery. They called themselves Luddites after the mythical Ned Ludd, who was supposed to have been an eighteenth-century saboteur who, like Robin Hood, had been rumoured to live in Sherwood Forest. The Luddites wrote letters and petitions signed King Ludd or General Ludd.

The word "saboteur" has an interesting history. In English, it has been used from early in the nineteenth century to mean someone who deliberately destroys machinery or bridges to thwart an enemy. However, in French, it was common much earlier to liken a slow and clumsy worker to someone wearing wooden shoes, or sabots. In 1897, French anarchist Émile Pouget recommended that workers engage in a work slowdown, which he called "sabotage," to protest the use of labour-saving technology.

When Gutenberg introduced his press, there were no doubt people mourning the loss of jobs for scribes, and the invention of the wheel probably caused consternation among the bearers who would no longer be in such demand. The speed of technological change has increased dramatically, but its effect on the number of jobs has not changed. Technology changes over time, and each technological change has brought more jobs, new opportunities and economic growth than it destroyed. Those displaced by the changes suffered; it has never been easy to switch from old ways of doing things to new opportunities. In every instance, the people who mourned the loss of a way of life resisted the changes and imagined that the world was ending. And in every case, there was still plenty of work for human beings to do.

As a species, we are not very good at imagining the real changes that the future will bring, and we have always focused more on what we are losing than on what we are about to gain. There will be changes, but one change we need not fear is the elimination of work.

Imagining a Future Without Work Is Not New

We have always faced disruptive technological change, and we have always had visionaries imagining a society based on physical labour transformed into one in which human beings would no longer have to undertake the danger and drudgery of hard work to feed their families. Freed from backbreaking toil, they could exercise their individual human talents for art, music, philosophy and scholarship.

John Maynard Keynes is well-known today for championing a set of policies that highlighted the important role that a government can play in ensuring that the economy does not fall into a prolonged depression. He is less well remembered for a small book published in 1930, titled *Economic Opportunities for our Grandchildren*. In it, he predicted that within a hundred years — that is, by 2030 — living standards in industrialized countries would be between four and eight times higher than they were when he wrote. And, in fact, his estimate was modest if anything. Productivity grew far more quickly than he imagined. Where Keynes went spectacularly wrong was in how he expected us to adapt to our greater wealth. He predicted that we would reduce our work week to perhaps fifteen hours and share the necessary labour required to produce what we consume. The rest of our time we would spend improving ourselves through education, art and friendship.

Instead, we decided that we'd rather just consume a whole lot more than take our increased wealth in the form of leisure. North American working hours have remained more or less steady for decades, and we work 30 per cent more than Europeans. Workers can't be convinced to take their full vacation entitlement. European workers are now under increasing pressure from their governments to increase the hours they work, and efforts are underway in many countries to raise the age at which a worker can receive a state pension.

Nineteenth-century philosopher and economist John Stuart Mill is best remembered today as a reformer and a classical liberal. He championed free markets but recognized that the state had a role to play in limiting working hours and ensuring that workers were protected on job sites. He fought successfully to extend the vote to working men and, less successfully, to all women. He championed a woman's right to own property, to work and to divorce. He was active in antislavery circles.

Mill also imagined that capitalism was a necessary, but not ideal, stage in historical development. He believed that only capitalism could have generated the wealth that Britain had achieved by the nineteenth century, but he was well aware of its limitations. He imagined that the end of capitalism as it existed in the nineteenth century was just beyond the horizon and that, having worked so hard to create an economy that could generate such wealth, people were just about ready to enjoy their rewards in the form of increased time to spend on the finer things in life. In *Principles of Political Economy*, he wrote, "I confess I am not charmed with the ideal of life held out by those who think the normal state of human beings is that of struggling to get on; that the trampling, crushing, elbowing, and treading on each other's heels, which form the existing type of social life, are the most desirable lot of human kind, or anything but the disagreeable symptoms of one of the phases of industrial progress."[8]

Mill recognized that economic growth was not endless and believed that the real problem facing nineteenth-century Britain was that existing wealth should be better distributed: "I know not why it should be a matter of congratulation that persons who are already richer than anyone needs to be, should have doubled their means of consuming things which give little or no pleasure except as representative of wealth."[9] Economic growth for its own sake was unnecessary. A far better alternative would be to focus on the "art of living" — education, philosophy, music, friendship — which would be more easily pursued when less energy was devoted to work.

Even the father of modern economics, Adam Smith, recognized the dangers of overwork. He wrote *On the Wealth of Nations* in 1776, and one of his most well-known passages involves a description of the division of labour in a pin factory, in which one man straightens the wire, another cuts it and so on. Through the co-operation of labour within the factory system, efficiency is increased and output increases dramatically. But even Smith recognized the consequences of too great a reliance on the division of labour. When every worker has only a simple task to perform, he has no time or inclination to consider any ideas beyond those immediately connected to his employment. According to

Smith, this leads to poor outcomes for the individual as well as society at large.[10]

The post-work utopia imagined by Silicon Valley executives may seem like science fiction, but most good science fiction is rooted not solely in imagination, but in the ideas of the present and the past. So, too, are the ideas that technology is disruptive, that it will lead to a world beyond work, and that this post-work world might be a significant improvement over the current situation.

A More Realistic Story

So: are we heading into a period of labour shortages in which we must adopt policies to force as many people as possible to work longer and harder, or are we heading into a world where jobs will be scarce because machines produce all we can possibly need or want? As it has throughout history, technology will disrupt the current state of society. It will cause shortages of some kinds of labour while other workers struggle to find jobs. In total, technology will create more jobs than it will destroy. The real issue is one particularly suited to basic income: technology will affect the quality of the jobs available, and the rise of precarious labour will force us to think about how we deliver social policies.

Without question, we are facing labour shortages for particular kinds of labour. There are skill mismatches in some high-technology areas, which tend to drive wages in these sectors very high, effectively turning the market for highly educated labour international and this kind of labour into a highly prized (and highly priced) commodity. No amount of legislation designed to keep sixty-five-year-olds working for a few more years as Walmart greeters, and no rules requiring the unemployed to show that they have actively searched for work, will solve this problem. It is a matter of the supply of these kinds of labour lagging behind demand in rapidly evolving sectors. One obvious solution is to raise wages so that people are attracted to these sectors and willing to work to gain the skills necessary for such highly paid jobs. And this is what markets do — and do very well. We don't need social policies or government regulations to address labour shortages for highly skilled and highly priced workers.

At the other end of the wage scale, there are also labour shortages. It is increasingly difficult for firms to find Canadians willing to do hard physical labour at low wages in agriculture, to find minimum-wage workers for the service industry (especially in locations where the housing market is booming), or to hire unskilled workers in the low-waged, non-unionized construction sector. One response would be to offer higher wages and better working conditions, which might attract workers, and this is how a market would work. An alternative that is increasingly feasible is to automate. Again, left to itself, the market does a pretty good job of eliminating labour shortages by allowing wages to increase and encouraging automation when it would pay off.

And yet, some aspects of current economic change are profoundly different from the past. Even if technological change brings with it new opportunities, it also will cause significant disruptions. While there is no shortage of jobs, the kinds of jobs that are on offer are rapidly changing and will not necessarily match well with the skills of the people who need work. It is no easy task to turn the pharmacists displaced by pill-counting robots into app developers, and it is even more difficult to re-employ the people laid off from factory work or resource industries as caregivers. Increasingly, the new jobs that are created will not look anything like the jobs of the past and will require significant and extensive retraining.

Even when the work to be done is unchanged, the ways in which people are hired to do that work have changed. Instead of hiring someone into a career position and committing to that person for the long term, employers are more likely to seek contract workers who can be hired and let go on demand. The trend toward precarious and contingent employment is already well entrenched, and technological changes will enhance this shift. Global competition has heightened the desire on the part of Canadian firms to reduce labour costs. At the same time, new technologies make feasible new types of contingent work. Carl Benedikt Frey and Michael A. Osborne found that 47 per cent of US employment is at high risk of being automated in the next twenty years.[11] Creig Lamb replicated Frey and Osborne's study for the Canadian economy and estimated that 42 per cent of employment in Canada is at high risk.[12]

A recent report by the federal government documented the range of job types in existence and the general movement toward less and less stable types of work contracts.[13] Traditionally, unskilled and semi-skilled workers such as taxi drivers and food delivery personnel have been especially vulnerable to work outsourcing through online platforms such as Uber and SkipTheDishes, but the rise of new virtual platforms threatens even middle-class jobs. As technology becomes increasingly integrated into our work, complex careers such as accounting, law or pharmacy require less skill on the part of those who undertake some of the work. Large parts of the work of community pharmacists can be replaced by pill-dispensing robots. As the software becomes more sophisticated, larger parts of many professional jobs become less demanding.[14] Professional careers increasingly turn into lower-skilled full-time or part-time jobs undertaken by legal assistants and paralegals, bookkeepers and pharmacy technicians. A firm with a new contract might hire freelancers as contractors for a fixed term and then release them when the project is complete. Potential contractors face competition not only from Canadians, but from workers all over the world who can access the new online platforms. This competition has dramatic effects on international income distribution. Skilled workers from low-wage countries can now access higher-paying jobs offered by firms located in high-income countries while workers in high-income countries face new competition for work they used to assume was theirs by right.

Translators, for example, who used to have relatively good access to permanent jobs with reasonable incomes, now find themselves in competition with contractors from all over the world, not to mention machine translations that are improving rapidly. Newspaper columnists are a dying species, and journalists of all types find themselves cobbling together an income from a series of less secure contracts and jobs. A variety of online platforms (or websites) bring together those who have projects to be completed with those eager for work, and the number of participants is staggering:

- Upwork (nine million freelancers)

- Freelancer (sixteen million freelancers)

- Hourly Nerd (over ten thousand MBA graduates from top schools)

- ProZ (766,603 translators)

- Fiverr (over three million service providers)

There are also websites for those willing to take on even shorter-term, less demanding tasks for much less money. Workers can supplement their incomes by completing microtasks — anything from accessing a website to completing a survey — that pay as little as five cents a task through online platforms like Amazon's Mechanical Turk. Cloudflower, a similar platform, has over five million contributors.

As long as decisions to participate in such activities are a choice and not a necessity, they provide a valuable opportunity for potential employees. These platforms offer opportunities for creatively balancing the necessity of work with the freedom to allocate time to other activities such as travel, education, creativity or leisure. Many platform workers are young people who are also engaged in education, and these work arrangements allow them the flexibility to combine their various commitments. However, for some people, part-time work or platform work is oppressive. They would prefer full-time, standard jobs that, because of the rapidly changing job market, they cannot find or cannot keep.

Technological change is disruptive, and it will have important consequences that basic income solves very well. Basic income can make life easier for people whose jobs have disappeared and who cannot easily retrain for new opportunities. Basic income can supplement the incomes of people whose jobs have been transformed by technology from full-time careers into contingent and low-paying piecework. However, technology will not eliminate the need for human labour.

Chapter 5
Work and Human Dignity

Mincome hired dozens of young graduates from the Universities of Manitoba and Winnipeg to interview recipients and collect data. I spoke with one of the most respected sociologists working in Canada today, who had his first exposure to social science research as a Mincome interviewer. He told me a story that still moves him almost forty years later. He went to visit one of the Mincome families living in the rural municipality surrounding Dauphin and pulled up in front of a small house on a very marginal farmstead. Used to deprivation by this point, he steeled himself for what he might find within. He was welcomed and ushered into the front room to wait for tea and dainties.[1] Taking pride of place, a polished, oversized wooden stereo console occupied one long wall, surrounded by shelves and shelves of records — the largest classical music and opera collection he had ever seen. Noticing his interest, the owner began to explain how the collection had been gathered and cared for over many years, and how she and her husband had raised their children in a home poor by many standards, but always rich in music and literature. She laughed as she told him how everything stopped at noon on Saturdays, so they could listen to the radio together — *Saturday Afternoon at the Opera* on CBC.

I think one of the reasons that story resonates is because it reminds us of the richness and variety of human experience. People do their best to live their lives in ways that affirm their individuality. Any "rational" consideration of that story might suggest that indoor plumbing should have been a greater priority than a music collection, but it would be hard to argue that the family had made an uninformed decision. Yet we often do a very poor job of recognizing human variation, and, as a result, our analysis of how a basic income might affect our lives is quite naive.

Why Do People Work?

One of the great fears that many critics bring to a discussion of basic income is that people will work less if they can get money from a basic income for doing nothing. This is an important consideration because if enough people work less, the cost of running a basic income program, and the burden on taxpayers, will be greater than expected. At the same time, a significant reduction in work effort will also reduce the growth of Canadian productivity and, consequently, the growth of tax revenue that could be used to pay for the program. That is, if people work less, basic income becomes more expensive at the same time that our ability to pay for it is constrained. There is also a moral issue involved: most of us believe that working is good for people.

Economists like to talk about "incentivizing labour" — making work pay. This is based on the assumption that the only reason anyone works is because we bribe them with money to do something they would not otherwise choose to do. If we want them to work harder, we have to offer them higher wages. If we cut their take-home pay through higher taxation, they will work fewer hours or work less hard and produce less during the hours they do work. There is, however, very little evidence to support this claim, and a great deal of evidence to suggest that the reasons people work are as varied as the people themselves.

The decision to work for money is actually three separate decisions: first, people have to decide whether or not to look for a job; second, if offered a job, they need to decide whether or not to accept it; and third, if they take a job, they sometimes have to make a decision about how many hours they will work or how hard they will work. The first two decisions — whether to look for a job and whether to accept a job — are influenced by many factors, of which the amount of money they will bring home is only one:

> Shaun Loney is the founder of half a dozen or more social enterprises in Manitoba, often in partnership with First Nations. One of his projects is bedbug mitigation. Shaun hires people at minimum wage to do a job few of us would take on at any wage. He never struggles to find willing workers. The people Shaun hires are people with personal demons — many sport prison tattoos, and almost all have had some involvement in the drug trade. Literacy and basic job skills are issues, as are addictions. Most need many second chances. When Shaun spreads the word that he has work to offer, people line up to apply. Applicants are not applying for these jobs because they expect to enjoy the work. The monetary reward is limited, particularly since it means his workers lose provincial income assistance. So why do people work? Some work for Shaun because he arranges opportunities for them to acquire a driver's licence. Others know that he offers literacy training, and (for some) opportunities to gain access to trades. Others work because they know that too little structure in their days will lead them back into trouble they are working hard to escape. Some enjoy the camaraderie of the bedbug brigade. Still others are proud to be a role model for their children, or their nieces and nephews. The wage is very often the least of it.

> Aaliyah is a foley artist. She adds sound effects after production to a wide range of film, video and other media — everything from the rustling of leaves to the swishing of

clothing to the breaking of glass. We met when she came to record the different moods of my honeybees for her sound library. She has worked on contract for museums, trying to create immersive experiences, and for film and television projects. In the summer, she is on a tree-planting crew in northern British Columbia, and the rest of the year she supplements her income working as a server in an upscale restaurant. When I asked her how a basic income might affect her life, she said, "You know, this works for me. I'd like to say I'd cut back on the restaurant work to focus on my art, but really, I like serving. And tree-planting is really hard work, but I feel so good to be out there. All the bits fit together pretty nicely. Probably I'd just feed my habit — buy more sound equipment."

In the 2017 *World Happiness Report*, a group of economists and psychologists surveyed people from all over the world to find out how happy they were — whether they believed themselves to be happy or depressed, and how they evaluated their lives overall.[2] The report found that people who were employed scored higher on "positive affect,"[3] lower on "negative affect" and higher on overall "life evaluation"[4] than people who were not employed. Our first response might be to dismiss these results; after all, people who are employed are more likely to have money than people who are unemployed, and, with money, they can afford to build more comfortable lives and probably have more stable families. However, even when we compare people who are the same age and sex and have the same family income, the unemployed still report significantly less well-being than those with full-time employment. It is not just the money associated with employment that seems to bring satisfaction. These results are important because how long we live, how well we function and how healthy we are overall is associated with how satisfying we find our lives.[5]

Not all jobs are equal, to be sure. Some characteristics of jobs are associated with improved well-being: higher wages, job security, autonomy, the opportunity to learn new things, support from others on the job and opportunities for advancement. Other characteristics reduce perceived well-being: job insecurity, dirty or dangerous work, lack of control, jobs that interfere with family time and worry about work outside job hours.

There are some important things to notice, though. In general, people who find the kind of job arrangement that they want are happiest. For example, in high-income countries, self-employed people are happier than those with full-time employment. Presumably, self-employment gives them the opportunity for greater autonomy and control over their time. In low-income countries, however, self-employment is often less about controlling your own life than about mere survival; it is often the employment of last resort, and it's not surprising that many people in such circumstances would prefer a regular, full-time job. All employment variables matter more for men than for women. Women who voluntarily work part-time are happier than those working full-time. Involuntary part-time employment and being out of the labour force are associated with lower levels of happiness, especially for men.

On a less theoretical level, we know that people value work because of how hard they work to find a job when there is no material advantage to doing so. Most food banks in Canada rely on volunteer labour, and the volunteers are disproportionately people with lived experience of poverty. Many are not in the labour force because of disabilities or mental health issues that make it difficult to keep a job even though they might not qualify for disability support. Working at the food bank does not increase their entitlement to a food basket; they get one whether they work or not. It does not earn them any other material rewards except, perhaps, a modest lunch and a bus ticket. The work can be hard and dusty; there are not many opportunities to perfect high-level skills. However, no food bank has difficulty attracting volunteers from among its clients. People value the job. Their reasons vary: some like the social aspects of work while others want to feel useful.

Work helps to structure our lives. People feel better about themselves and about their lives when they work, and this is true not only of high-paying professional jobs with autonomy, but also of many low-skilled and physically demanding jobs. Most people like to work. These results are consistent with all we know about the positive effects of work on human well-being. A 2014 meta-analysis found strong evidence that employment protects individuals against depression and reduces psychological stress. Employment is associated with better mental health.[6]

Some people who have decided to accept a job must then make another decision about how many hours they will work. For those in standard jobs, there is often little choice: many jobs do not allow workers to voluntarily reduce their hours (and pay) without losing benefits and opportunities. Some jobs allow overtime, but whether to accept it is often not entirely under the control of the worker. However, the labour market is changing in such a way that many of us can find a second job or "side hustle" that offers us the opportunity to work a few more hours for more money. How do people decide how many hours to work? Whether they realize it or not, they probably weigh the benefits of working an additional hour against the costs of working that hour. The benefits include how much more money they will bring home after taxes of all types, and the costs include things such as additional childcare, transportation, and so on. Many of the benefits and costs, however, are not monetary: costs include time away from family and reduced opportunities to engage in unpaid volunteer, creative or care work. A non-monetary benefit might include the opportunity to learn particular skills, or to build relationships with colleagues or contacts. The satisfaction of doing a job someone considers important and meaningful will influence how many hours to work, as will the praise received from a skilled employer. People are different and will be influenced by different factors.

Dan Ariely is a behavioural economist at Duke University and the author of *Predictably Irrational*. In a series of experiments, Ariely explores how we make decisions and shows that human beings are often less rational than economists sometimes assume. He investigates the question of what motivates us to work, and, using two ingenious experiments, shows us that work is not motivated solely by money, but it isn't motivated by the pleasure of the work itself either. In one experiment, participants were given a simple building task using Legos and asked if they were prepared to undertake the task for $3.00. If they agreed, the experimenter accepted the result, set it on the table and offered the participant a second opportunity to build for $2.75. If they agreed, they were offered a third opportunity at a lower price, and so on. Then the experiment was repeated with different participants, but this time the experimenter disassembled the product of the first round as the builder was completing the second. The participants were prepared to build more creations at a lower price when the experimenter accepted the result than when the experimenter destroyed the result. The pay offered to the participant was unchanged, but the futility of the task was made much clearer in the second case. In a second experiment, participants were given the opportunity to make origami creations. In one trial, participants were given good instructions, and then they were given the opportunity to "buy" the results of their labour. The participants valued the products they created more than did others who, presumably, had a more objective view of their quality. In a second trial, the participants were given poor instructions. The results were demonstrably worse than in the first trial, but participants valued the results even more — presumably because of the extra effort required to complete the task.

Most of us, Ariely concluded, work harder and longer when we can see that we are making constant progress and feel a sense of purpose in our work.[7] Focusing too narrowly on take-home pay often leads us to draw unwarranted conclusions.

Notwithstanding all of these insights, the debate about whether people offered a basic income would work fewer hours tends to ignore everything except money.

The Effects of a Basic Income on the Amount of Work People Do

There is no perfect evidence that will tell us how people will behave when a basic income is introduced. Experiments were conducted in North America during the 1970s precisely to understand whether people would work less. However, these were short-term experiments, and all participants knew they were temporary. People might behave differently when a program is generally available and expected to be permanent, than when they participate in a temporary experiment. We do know that when offered a basic income in a temporary experiment, the reduction in work effort was quite modest.

Five negative income tax experiments took place in North America in the 1970s — four in the United States and Mincome in Canada. The first American experiment was conducted on an urban population in New Jersey and Pennsylvania between 1968 and 1972.[8] A second experiment was conducted in Gary, Indiana, to examine the effect of a basic income on single parents.[9] A third took place in North Carolina and Iowa to look at the effects on rural populations.[10] The final experiment was the Seattle-Denver Income Maintenance Experiment (SIME/DIME), which had access to a much larger experimental population.[11] The four US experiments used a carefully selected experimental sample and randomized participants into treatment and control groups. They collected quantitative and qualitative data from both subjects and controls, and experimenters hoped that comparing the experiences of those who received the basic income to the control group would allow them to determine the effects of a basic income on a wide variety of social behaviours. The Winnipeg site of the Canadian experiment followed the same structure, but the Dauphin site was the only saturation site in any of the North American experiments that offered a basic income to all qualifying participants in the site.

Details of the experiments are summarized in Table 5.1.

Table 5.1   Summary of the Features of the North
American Income Maintenance Experiments

Parameter	New Jersey	Rural (RIME)	Seattle-Denver (SIME/DIME)	Gary	Mincome
Site	Trenton, Patterson-Passaic, and Jersey City, N.J.; Scranton, Pa.	Duplin County, N.C; Pocahontas and Calhoun Counties, Iowa	Seattle, Wash., Denver, Colo.	Gary, Ind.	Winnipeg and Dauphin, Manitoba
Eligibility	Intact households headed by able-bodied males 18-58 with at least one dependent and incomes < 150 per cent of poverty line	Families with at least one dependent and incomes < 150 per cent of poverty line	Families with at least one dependent and incomes < $11,000 (singleheaded) or $13,000 (double headed)	Black households, head 18-58 with at least one dependent and income < 240 per cent of poverty line	Families with able-bodied heads under 58 years old, incomes < $13,000 (family of four)
Sample Size	1,357 households; 725 experimentals, 632 controls	809 families: 587 non-aged male-headed, 108 non-aged female-headed, 114 older heads	4,801 families (Denver 2,758, Seattle 2,043)	1,800 black households, 60 per cent female-headed (125 households added with incomes above 240 per cent of poverty line)	1,300 families and single individuals
Plans [not all t, G combinations included in each experiment; more generous plans (high G, low t) typically excluded]	8 plans; t = .3, .5, .7; G = .5, .75, 1.0, 1.25 of poverty line ($5,000 for family of 4)	8 plans t = .3, .5, .7; G = .5, .75, 1.0 of poverty line	11 plans; t = .5, .7, .7*, .8* (* indicates tax rate declines per .025 per $100 income); G = .95, 1.2, 1.4 of poverty line; training counseling, training subsidies (50 per cent, 100 per cent)	4 plans; t = .4, .6; G = .75, 1.0 of poverty line, social services counseling, day care subsidies (35 per cent, 60 per cent, 80 per cent)	Winnipeg; 7 plans; t = .35, .5, .75; G = $3,800, 4,800, 5,800 (family of four in 1975) Dauphin: 1 plan (saturated site); t = .5; G = $3,800
Duration (start-up date)	3 years/1968-69	3 years/1970	3, 5 years, 20 years (Denver only)/1969	3 years/1971	3 years/1975

Note: t refers to the experimental tax rate; G refers to the experimental income guarantee rate.

Source: Derek Hum and Wayne Simpson, "Economic response to a guaranteed annual income: Experience from Canada and the United States," *Journal of Labor Economics* 11, no. 1, part 2: U.S. and Canadian Income Maintenance Programs (1993): S275.

The researchers hoped that the experiments would throw light on all kinds of social behaviours, but the experiments were designed specifically to illuminate one set of decisions. The fundamental purpose of all these experiments was to determine the impact of a basic income on the supply side of the labour market: specifically, would people opt out of the labour market to subsist on benefits? Would those who continued to work choose to work fewer hours to optimize benefits? Overall, the results of the experiments were remarkably consistent. The results are summarized in Table 5.2.

Table 5.2   Annual Change In Hours Worked During North American Income Maintenance Experiments

Experiments	Husbands	Wives	Single Female Heads
Mincome	-20 (1 per cent)	-15 (3 per cent)	-56 (5 per cent)
New Jersey	-57 (3 per cent)	-62 (28 per cent)	
Rural	-93 (5 per cent)	-180 (28 per cent)	
Seattle-Denver	-135 (8 per cent)	-129 (20 per cent)	-134 (13 per cent)
Gary	-76 (5 per cent)	-18 (6 per cent)	-84 (23 per cent)
Overall US Results	-69 (6 per cent)	-70 (19 per cent)	-85 (15 per cent)

Source: Derek Hum and Wayne Simpson, "Whatever Happened to Canada's Guaranteed Income Project?" *Canadian Public Administration* 36, no. 3 (1993): 448.

The second column in Table 5.2 represents the effect of basic income on the number of hours worked by those most attached to the labour market — adult men. These were primary earners and their reaction to a basic income was, overall, quite modest. Men, for the most part, did not quit their jobs although the average number of hours worked did fall a small amount. The smallest average results occurred in Manitoba (an annual work reduction of less than half a week) and the largest in Seattle-Denver. However, these results represent average reductions in hours worked. Among men, the largest effects were on adolescents in all of the experiments. If we look at the results a bit closer, interesting effects become apparent. For example, Seattle-Denver had a combination of experimental designs underway, some of which included heavily subsidized or free job training. One of the significant results in that experiment was a positive effect on adult education. Did these men reduce their work hours because they received a basic income and they preferred not to work, or did they reduce their work hours to engage in job training or, as the researchers labelled it, to accumulate human capital? Certainly in Dauphin, reduced work effort among young males was associated with increased education.[12]

Basic income was associated with a larger reduction in work effort for women, but both the design and the context in which these results are produced needs to be taken into account. In the Canadian case, the results were very small overall with the largest reduction in work effort associated with single mothers. Women in all five sites, whether they were married women or single mothers, worked significantly fewer hours if they received a basic income. The percentage change is large, but what is most notable is how few hours married women worked even before they received a basic income. For example, in New Jersey, a 28 per cent reduction in work hours resulted in 62 fewer hours worked per year, which means that on average, these women were working about four hours per week before the experiment began. These experiments took place during the 1970s, when few women expected to work their entire lives. Women were just beginning to enter the workforce in large numbers, and many still did not consider their jobs an important part of their identity or even an important source of income for their families. If they did work out of necessity, it is unlikely that they had the training or the opportunity to access good full-time work. A reasonable response, under the circumstances, was for many of these women to opt out of paid work or reduce their hours to take care of their children. Most women today do not consider their earnings either secondary or expendable. They work for the same reason that men work — to pay their bills.[13]

These numbers illustrate a much more fundamental change in the ways that women and men and families organize their lives. These experiments took place at the beginning of a period of profound change in family organization. Men were still primary earners, and both spouses expected them to be. Lone mothers were more often widows than divorced or never married. Mothers of young children received income assistance, but there was little support for widows with grown children beyond savings or, in exceptional cases, survivor's pensions attached to their husbands' previous employment. During Mincome, especially in the Dauphin site, widows were in a particularly difficult position. There was no Guaranteed Income Supplement at that time, and many would have been too young for Old Age Security. There was no mature Canada Pension Plan in place, and many of their husbands would have been self-employed with little capacity to leave a large pension or insurance policy. When their husbands died, they found themselves with grown children but too old and unskilled to compete for a job and too young to collect a pension. They had never trained to work and never expected to do so. The introduction of a basic income for these women alleviated a great deal of hardship. Younger women were beginning to move into the labour market and to regard their work as more than a temporary period before motherhood or an opportunity to buy extras for their families. Yet older women were still living with a set of values and expectations forged in a period of male breadwinners and stay-at-home wives.

Overall, the results of the 1970s experiments suggest that people will not substantially reduce their hours worked. However, these experiments all had a definite end date that was known to participants. Those most likely to curtail their work in the experiments were precisely those making short term decisions: the older worker coasting into retirement, the young worker who knows that eventually a real job will be necessary but perhaps not quite yet, and the mother with preschool children who will not be infants forever. Those with longer perspectives had virtually no reaction. There is a problem generalizing about human behaviour from temporary experiments. We do not know how people will change their work behaviour if basic income becomes an established program. We can guess that those used to living a richer lifestyle will be hesitant about trading it for a modest basic income. We can assume that people who derive satisfaction and pleasure from their work will continue to work. We cannot, however, know with certainty how low-waged workers will behave when basic income is fully institutionalized — and no experiment can produce that knowledge.

There are other kinds of data we can look at to get some idea of how people would behave if a basic income were introduced. Czech economist Jitka Specianova examined survey data, data generated by economic modelling, the behaviour of lottery winners and laboratory experiments. The largest results were among lottery winners who received their winnings as an annual or monthly income, in almost all cases significantly larger than any proposed basic income. In general, lottery winners were likely to decrease the amount they worked, but the overall size of the effect was still small. The size of the response depended on the amount of the lottery winnings, the satisfaction people had with their current job, whether they perceived the job as a part of daily life, age, education, gender and status. That is, Jitka's results confirm the findings of Dan Ariely and others: many factors other than wages and taxes influence whether and how much people choose to work.[14]

There is little evidence that the introduction of a basic income will cause people to work substantially less overall, but there is some merit to allowing individuals the right to choose how much to work without coercing them to take whatever job they can find. Some people, particularly those in low-paid and unpleasant jobs, may choose to work less if they have access to a basic income. If the work they abandon is necessary work that must be done, their refusal to work will encourage employers to improve the terms of employment. If consumers will not buy the products at a price sufficient to hire enough labour to produce it, then those consumers will have made the decision to do without the product.

The ability of poorly paid and badly treated workers to reject demeaning work is not a problem to be solved; it is a benefit of basic income.

The Social Benefits of Working Less

A significant reduction in work hours overall is unlikely. However, it is worth considering whether a reduction in work hours is necessarily a negative outcome. North Americans work many more hours than people in most European nations, and since the 1970s, the increase in hours worked by women has broadened the gap.[15] We have begun to transform other social policies to reflect growing evidence that overwork is not necessarily beneficial. In Canada in the 1970s, the entitlement to maternity leave was four weeks. Since then, we have substantially increased paid and partially paid parental leave because we recognize the evidence that families benefit from the opportunity to spend more time together and to forge deeper bonds with newborns. Moreover, the leave is extended to men as well as to women because it is more than just an opportunity to heal from the physical trauma of birth. Young people are encouraged by all kinds of social policies to stay in school longer, to engage in training and to take their first jobs at a later date. More and more private firms are offering opportunities for sabbaticals, recognizing the benefit that comes from productive leisure. Is it necessarily a negative outcome to find that families will take some of their income — especially if their income is enhanced through a basic income — in the form of greater flexibility in their use of time? Some will engage in training and education; others will spend more time taking care of their own family members rather than paying others to provide necessary care. Some people might choose to spend time in creative or voluntary pursuits or to engage in innovative entrepreneurial activities. Others may just read more novels or go for an additional hike. The point is that wealthy societies can afford to take some of their wealth in the form of a greater quality of life associated with time away from paid labour.

Some work is important to the well-being of society but is not part of the paid labour market. Caregiving has never fit well into a formal labour market. Nursing homes are rarely preferred by patients over care provided by a family member. A mother at home with preschoolers today faces social pressure to justify her decision not to use daycare, but no one would argue that a society can survive and flourish without someone undertaking these activities. These services might be provided by someone we pay to do the work, or they might be provided by a family member for no pay, but society does require that this kind of work be done. A basic income is a way to value the unpaid work of caregivers. Similarly, creative work is essential to social well-being, but the market does a poor job of encouraging it. Long before the Industrial Revolution, artists required the income and support of patrons to assure their continued production. More recently, the state has provided pensions or grants to a small number of applicants. Both institutions recognize how significant creative work is, but neither encourages widespread creativity or supports all those who believe they have something worthwhile to say. Some artists and some caregivers may choose to subsist on a basic income and dedicate themselves to what they consider their important work rather than taking a job for pay. Whether we want to support a more robust creative sector and the freedom to choose whether or not to work for pay depends on the kind of society in which we want to live. If the cost of a basic income is the production of a little more poetry than the market would support, is that a bad thing?

There will no doubt be some people who choose not to engage in non-market production, volunteer labour or work for pay. If a basic income is provided without conditions, some people will do very little. Some will fish all day or daydream under an apple tree. This decision is a difficult one for people living in industrialized countries to accept, but the great philosophers of the past recognized the importance of leisure. Economists tend to identify leisure as any period not devoted to work for pay in the market, but philosophers have always had a more nuanced view. Aristotle pointed out that as soon as society had reached a level of output that would allow it to provide the necessities of life for everyone, people began to think about science and art. It is no accident, he claimed, that scientific progress occurred first in places where people had a reasonable amount of leisure time that they could use to think rather than simply work. Egypt, for example, is where mathematics first began to flourish, and it began among the priestly caste that was allowed time for leisure.

Almost all of the great achievements of past centuries in the arts, sciences, music, philosophy and scholarship were created by people who had, for all intents and purposes, the equivalent of a basic income. They were not people who worked for a wage, but rather members of aristocratic families who did not need to work for money, or talented individuals who had attracted a patron who could finance their leisure, or employees of the Church for (some of) whom "holy leisure" had always been part of a balanced life. Leisure — not mere relaxation or entertainment, but time and the ability to contemplate — is essential to the well-being and advancement of societies.

Contemporary philosopher Martha Nussbaum wrote *Creating Capabilities*, in which she argued that leisure is at least as unequally distributed in our world as is wealth and is at least as important for social progress. She imagines a young girl named Vasani in rural India, and wonders whether she ever has access to time just to sit and think, to enjoy something beautiful or to share tea with her friends. We might ask the same question about a harried single parent, rushing between daycare and two different jobs: what is the value of leisure?

Basic income not only offers everyone access to the resources to live a modest life; it offers to everyone the opportunity to participate in leisure. Not everyone will spend money the way I believe they ought to, and not everyone will spend time the way I think it ought to be spent. But I am not in a position to judge the priorities of other people. The fundamental characteristic of basic income is that everyone becomes the judge of how to spend his or her own time and money without the help and assistance of people who believe themselves to know better. In our culture, leisure may be the most difficult good to obtain. We are rich in money and resources. We struggle with too much food and too much waste. We are brought up from infancy to achieve, to make, to do. We are not encouraged to be visionaries and dreamers.

Reconsidering Our Attachment to the Labour Market

Not everyone is a caregiver or an artist, and not everyone aspires to be. With no work requirement, some people will nonetheless choose to work for pay because that is how they find human contact and satisfaction in their lives. Some will work for a wage or the inherent value of the work itself while others will work because they enjoy their colleagues or the routine of work. A few will decide that, on the whole, the job they are offered is not worth the low wage attached to it. They will either seek a different job, volunteer or do something else with their time. The job will then be done by someone who makes a different decision about the value of the wage and the nature of the job. If no one chooses to take the job at the wage offered, then either the wage will have to increase, or the job will not be done.

As economies grow and develop, many previously necessary jobs do disappear from the local labour market. Few people in North America or Europe have the households full of servants that earlier generations "needed" and that are still considered essential to middle-class life in places like India or Indonesia. Even the well off survive without the footmen and butlers that used to facilitate genteel lives. Farms in Europe and North America today do without much of the low-paid farm labour that characterized earlier agriculture. The very low-waged child labour of the first industrial revolution that was essential to the textile factories that drove economic growth is not a feature of high-income industrialized economies today. As certain types of labour become more expensive, either technology (such as washing machines and dishwashers) replaces formerly necessary workers, or we choose to do without the product of these labourers as we now do without small appliance repair. At some point, it becomes cheaper to replace the toaster than to hire someone to fix it.

A basic income encourages us to ask important questions about how we want to live our lives, how we value ourselves and each other, and how we will know whether our society is developing in directions that lead to better lives and greater opportunities. A basic income is not simply about eliminating poverty, but about extending the freedom to each of us to make these decisions for ourselves based on our own set of values.

Chapter 6
Women and Basic Income

The lives of Canadian women have changed fundamentally over the past fifty years. Our world is no longer one in which women and men play distinct roles, with men taking primary responsibility for supporting a family financially and women at home raising children, taking care of older or disabled family members and keeping a house. Dramatic social change never comes without anxiety. Many worry that the gains women have made in the labour market are fragile, and it would take little to undermine recent progress. Others fear that rapid change has costs that we have not taken into account, and that women still bear a disproportionate burden. Basic income acts as a lightning rod for such fears because it can affect our decisions about whether and how much to work for pay.

Labour economists such as Barbara Bergmann recognize the gains women have made in the labour market over the past fifty years and worry that the labour force participation rate of women seems to be stalling at levels lower than their male counterparts, suggesting that full gender equality is still elusive.[1] Others argue that women's lives are about more than their jobs and gender equality involves more than pay scales and professional opportunities. A basic income, they argue, could help to eliminate the power differentials between men and women that still subject too many women to poverty and violence.[2] Nested in the middle of this debate is a concern about caregiving: in Canada, as elsewhere in this world, women provide most of unpaid caregiving for children and the aged.[3] A basic income would compensate women for their work outside the market and provide the resources necessary to leave coercive personal relationships. But is the cost too high? Will a basic income encourage women to work less, and will this damage their lifetime earnings, their pension entitlements and their job achievements?[4]

Previous experiments can't contribute much to a discussion of gender today. The North American experiments took place during the 1970s, which was a long time ago insofar as gender relations are concerned. Mothers of preschoolers stayed at home except in the direst of financial circumstances, and even many school-aged children lived with stay-at-home mothers. Lone female parents were exceptional and usually the result of the early death of a spouse rather than divorce or unmarried parenthood. Male wages substantially exceeded female wages, so that even if a couple chose to make a "rational" decision about which one would work outside the home, there would be little to discuss. Similarly, generalizing from experiments in low- or middle-income countries with very different social expectations poses difficulties.

A basic income will have a profound effect on the lives of women just as it will transform the lives of men. However, different women will have very different needs, expectations and experiences. There are immense differences between the experiences and opportunities of different Canadian women, and understanding the impact of a basic income on women requires us to use enough imagination and empathy to recognize that education, culture, social class, ethnicity, race and geography matter at least as much as does gender. Basic income, however, works by offering people security and independence. While each will experience the effects of basic income differently, no adult can be made worse off by greater security and independence.

Basic Income, Work Gaps and Lifetime Consequences across the Income Spectrum

Today, 81.9 per cent of women are in the paid labour force (including 70 per cent of women with children less than three years old), compared with 90.5 per cent of men. Both adults report income in 96 per cent of two-adult families. Only 50.7 per cent of husbands earn more than their wives, while 32 per cent of couples rely equally on the earnings of both spouses, and 17.3 per cent of wives earn more than their husbands. As recently as 1985, 71.3 per cent of husbands earned more than their wives.[5] The increased participation of women in the paid labour market is accompanied by a smaller increase in the participation of men in household tasks. In 1986, women provided 75 per cent of household labour; in 2016, they still provided 61 per cent of household labour and 65 per cent of the hours spent caring for children.[6]

However, different women have very different experiences inside and outside the workplace. Choosing to stay at home with a young child has different consequences for a single mother than for a married woman. Someone with only a high school diploma or less will face different consequences than someone with a graduate degree.

Consider, first, the highly educated worker. According to Statistics Canada, approximately 300,000 mothers with a university degree who have children less than five years of age are not working for wages.[7] Of these, 200,000 are living with an adult partner. The decision to work or not to work will depend on many factors, but the availability of good quality daycare is no doubt one of them.[8] Another will be the existence of a high-earning partner to subsidize the family during a period out of work. Women who take time off work will consider the consequences of time outside the labour market, and these consequences will depend on the kind of job the mother might have held. For example:

> Yang is a university professor. Time off from work means
> slower career progress in the form of delayed tenure and
> promotion. The delay of a single year in promotion can have

a dramatic consequence on lifetime earnings. A professor is likely to have access to a pension plan. Time out of the work force reduces pension accumulation. When Yang returns to work, she will face colleagues on her promotion committee who will examine her publication track record, and some of them will wonder why she didn't use her parental leave to write a book or attend a conference while caring for a young child with no salary and no institutional support. In any case, her promotion will be delayed until she publishes enough to meet the promotion criteria. However, professorial work has many benefits, including sabbaticals and the opportunity to negotiate unpaid leaves. Professors have more control over their time than do many workers. Most universities have daycare centres that prioritize staff and students; daycare might be costly, but it is an investment. A professor facing the decision about whether to continue to work or to take time off to care for young children is in a very privileged position relative to most women, and few would argue that she is not capable of considering the consequences and making an informed decision.

Tooba, by contrast, is an associate at a top law firm. She is gunning for partner but finds the hours she is expected to bill incompatible with her childcare responsibilities. If she leaves the workforce, even for a short period, she will be penalized in terms of her career prospects when she tries to return. If she looks around for other opportunities, she will find that some legal jobs are far less demanding than the one she holds. She may well decide to take a salaried job in a corporation, or to become a professor at a law school or to otherwise move to the "mommy track" that affords her lower career horizons. Her lifetime income will be much lower than it might have been had she stayed at her previous job, as will her retirement savings. Her family life would certainly be less stressful. The decision she will make is not obvious, and it will certainly be a conflicted choice for many women. However, few would argue that this woman is incapable of making an informed decision.

Lindsay is an administrator in a firm. Her diploma affords her a reasonable salary and good benefits. Government and firm-level parental benefits offer her generous leave when her child is born, and her employer offers a few days each year for health and family care responsibilities. The cost of daycare may be significant and cause her to reconsider her job at times. If she does choose to leave her job, she is confident that her documented skills and good references will find her a new job when her child is a few years older. After all, many women work in this kind of job, and parental decisions, stressful as they are for individual families, are a well-understood part of career progress. Time off work with a young child will have an impact on her lifetime earnings and ultimately her pension, but she faces a fairly flat career path. Not many people become vice-president, so delayed promotions will matter less to her than to some women in different kinds of jobs. Again, there is no reason to assume that she is incapable of considering the consequences and making a decision.

These three well-educated women might make different decisions about continuing to work when their children are young because their careers are very different from one another. Their personal lives might also be quite different. An educated mother with a similarly well-educated partner has additional support both for the direct work of parenting and in financial terms. A university degree is no guarantee of economic well-being, but most married women with university degrees will be living with a partner who also has a good salary.[9] Whether she takes time off work to stay home with a young child will not be affected by basic income because her family income will be too high to qualify whether she works or not. The decisions these families make will depend on how each partner values his or her work, their relative wages and job circumstances, and the particular value that each partner places on the opportunity to spend more time with a young child. Either parent might decide to spend more time with a young child, and, depending on particular circumstances, either parent might have greater flexibility on the job or face fewer costs associated with time off work.

One thing that we can be fairly certain about is that a basic income will have little impact on the decisions of these highly educated women. If one parent takes time off work and their partner earns a professional salary, they will not qualify for any support. If a mother is single or her partner is paid little, she will decide whether to stay at home with a young child based on her job circumstances, the circumstances faced by her partner and the availability of good quality, affordable daycare. The basic income is unlikely to be enough in itself to induce the decision to stay home.

> Now, think about Chantal. She doesn't have a university degree or even a college diploma. Nevertheless, she has a good job at a manufacturing plant with a moderate salary and a union to negotiate benefits. Again, her parental benefits will allow her a long leave when her baby is born and adequate time off for family issues. Daycare will be a concern; is high-quality daycare at reasonable prices available? She has no partner to share childcare responsibilities. Depending on the availability of childcare, she might decide to stay home with her child or to continue to work. If she stays home, her future prospects are not likely to be much affected. During her period at home, she will benefit from the basic income. When she decides to go back to work, her future income and job prospects will not be much affected by the gap in her résumé.

Finally, imagine Darlene's life as a minimum-wage worker. Her job is not professional; it is not even full-time. She works two jobs with unpredictable hours, and, in the absence of a union, she has no access to generous leave policies or other benefits. She may or may not qualify for parental leave from Employment Insurance when her child is born; much depends on how many work hours she can get in the coming months. If she chooses to work, she will leave a very young infant to work at a job in which the hours do not coincide with those of most daycare centres. She might be forced to use private daycare, the quality of which varies. She has a partner, but he does not earn much more than she does, and his hours are equally unpredictable. If she were offered a basic income, she might well decide to stay at home. She would be better off financially than she would be in a minimum-wage job that requires her to pay for daycare. When her child goes to school, and she goes back to work, the gap in her work history will not hurt her prospects. She was not headed to the corner office before she decided to take time off work, and she is not likely to get there afterwards.

If we consider the variety of women's experiences in the labour market, it becomes clear that some women in all wage categories will decide to stay home with young children. For a high-waged woman, the deciding factor is likely to be the nature of the job, which will determine the personal consequences of her time away from work. If the personal costs are high and the job flexible, as in the case of a professor, she is not likely to take time off work. If the personal costs are high but the job inflexible, like the lawyer, she might decide that a work gap is worth the risk. If the personal costs are low, she might or might not take time off work depending on the nature of the job and the availability of daycare. High-income married women are unlikely to qualify for basic income even if they don't work because their family income will still be too high to qualify. Women without a partner might decide to rely on basic income when they have young children, depending on the circumstances of their employment and the availability of daycare. Whatever decisions they make, there is no reason to assume that they are unaware of the consequences in terms of future earnings and job prospects.

For low-waged women, the stakes are different. The availability of a basic income may well induce some low-waged women to stop working when they have young children at home. This is especially the case if daycare is unavailable or very expensive, or the hours of the job either unpredictable or inconsistent with daycare schedules. Staying home might even make some families better off financially, since their basic income will increase and their costs, including the cost of childcare, will decline. This is especially the case for single women or women with low-waged partners. Few of these women will suffer personal consequences from a gap in their work history. If all they can aspire to is minimum-wage work before they give birth, that work will still be available to them when the child is older. Years of minimum-wage work might lead to slightly better paying work, but it is not very likely to lead to the sorts of promotions and career progress higher-waged women take for granted. Periods of time out of work will affect high-waged, highly educated women a great deal but will have much less impact on low-waged women.

Gender, Unpaid Work and the Power Gap

Gender equality is about more than earnings capacity. It is about the ability of women to make their needs known in the halls of power and to assert their authority and wisdom in business and government. It is also about sharing equitably the unpaid care work that helps society to function. Many have speculated about how a basic income might affect the gender norms that govern society.[10] The division of labour, both paid and unpaid, between men and women is governed by a variety of factors including simple biology, the complex set of social norms that have evolved over centuries and the specific policy context in which decisions are made. It would be unreasonable to expect any single policy, including basic income, to bring about profound changes in gender relations on its own. However, gender norms do change, and they sometimes change very rapidly.

Some tasks will always fall to women as long as women continue to give birth. The actual physical labour of birth itself will always interrupt women's careers. This, however, is much less significant than decisions made within the family and within society about how to care for infants. The assumption that a mother's care is necessary in the early months and years of life is based not only on gender norms, but also on whether society organizes itself to make available appropriate parental leave and childcare at reasonable prices to share the task of raising infants with new mothers. Among couples who choose to have one parent stay at home, there are economic benefits for the highest earner to continue working for pay. While the proportion of wives who out-earn their husbands is growing rapidly, most male parents still earn more than female parents.[11] Among single parents, the decision about whether to work depends less on power dynamics and social norms than it does on the range of social policies available, including affordable daycare and income replacement.

A basic income alone will not change the world. However, there are ways to deliver a basic income that help to equalize power relationships in society and within the family. Even if a basic income is calculated on the basis of total family income, the lower-earning spouse might be the one who receives the money. This is a common decision in Canadian social policy that began with federal family allowances in the post-war period and continued through various forms of child benefits. The extent to which basic income can actually offset complex power differentials is debatable, but the knowledge that for at least one day a month, there will be income available to a person with no other dependable source of income is profound.

When we consider the potential impact of a basic income on women's lives, however, we need to remember that gender roles evolve over a lifetime. Much attention is paid to mothers of young children, particularly single mothers, and rightly so because the poverty rate among this group of Canadians is substantial. In 2015, 38.2 per cent of children under eighteen living with a single parent lived in poverty.[12] While the recent introduction of the Canada Child Benefit should help, the reality is that income assistance rates are simply too low to allow single mothers to raise their children. Only 12.4 per cent of children under eighteen living with two adults live in poverty. Clearly a basic income will help parents, especially single parents, with young children.

However, children eventually grow up, and most of the mothers who do not work when their children are preschoolers do enter the labour force and become wage-earners and taxpayers. But there are many reasons a woman might leave the labour force again, even after her children are grown. She might be called upon to provide care for an infirm spouse or parent, or a grown child or grandchild with health issues might need assistance beyond that available through public programs. Women's careers are marked by more and longer periods out of the labour force than are men's careers, and only some of these gaps relate to childbirth.[13]

Many adults are dependent on the earnings of a partner to share the cost of living. An adult unfortunate enough to live alone faces a substantial risk of poverty; 29 per cent of adults under sixty-five who live alone live in poverty. Among seniors, the poverty rate rises to 32 per cent for singles, but seniors living with a partner face the lowest poverty rate of any family type — 7.7 per cent — thanks to the Old Age Security pension and the Guaranteed Income Supplement.[14] While the Guaranteed Income Supplement rates for single people over age sixty-five have lagged behind the cost of living, the rates for couples are more generous. Recent decisions to adjust the Guaranteed Income Supplement and tie it to the cost of living will reduce the poverty rate among single adults over age sixty-five and reinforce the benefits of an adequate, dependable source of income.

A Basic Income Is a Source of Autonomy and Respect

Money plays many roles in society, but one of its most important features is that it is a source of autonomy and power. The autonomy might be obvious: an individual with money can buy exactly what she wants, when she wants it and from whomever she likes. She can go to Whole Foods or the local farmers' market, or she can shop at Price Chopper or the local corner store. She can buy organic carrots, milk, candy or even cigarettes. She may decide to divert a little of the budget to buy nail polish for three dollars at Dollarama. An independent woman can spend her money exactly as she likes. It is a matter of autonomy not to be told, implicitly or explicitly, that she does not have enough sense to know when she can afford to buy her son hot chocolate at Tim Hortons, or whether a new pair of pantyhose for a job interview might be more important. It is her money, and her decision.

The power associated with a basic income might be a bit less obvious. An individual with an adequate, secure and predictable income can make decisions that someone without such an income might find difficult. Several years ago, when I first began working with low-income women, I was astonished at how quickly any conversation about income assistance turned to the fear of having their children taken into care. I think many of us imagine that the reasons for child apprehension — abuse and neglect — are somehow independent of our income, and we can all remember or point to wonderful parents who raised successful children on very limited means. However, if you follow for a day a single mother of young children who receives income assistance and ask her to describe the decisions she is making, the connection between poverty and powerlessness becomes much clearer.

One example of the poor parental decision making that can draw the attention of authorities is leaving children unsupervised. How can a mother leave preschoolers at home alone? Suppose you have two children in diapers, and the laundromat is on the corner. If they were napping, would you leave for ten minutes to take a load out of the washing machine and put it in the dryer? Or would you wait for them to wake up, put on their snowsuits and walk them down the street, trying to keep them safe and supervised while dealing with the laundry? For parents with a partner, an apartment with a washing machine or the money to pay a babysitter, the issue never arises. How old is old enough to babysit? Would you leave them for twenty minutes with an older child? A ten-year-old? How about a seven-year-old, when you know that seven-year-old regularly walks to and from school alone, crossing busy streets and negotiating a challenging neighbourhood? (And if you are the mother of that seven-year-old, you may be in trouble on that account, as well.)

It is not always bad decisions that draw attention to the well-being of children. Your children, like my children, do silly things. They fall down and bruise themselves; they get into fights with one another. They fall off bikes and end up with bandages. Most teachers and principals know that children get banged up and never think to question the reported source of the injury. If your children also go to school when they have colds, runny noses and earaches because you have to work, it will be remembered. If you do not attend parent-teacher meetings because you are working odd hours, or perhaps because you are uncomfortable with the authority structures in schools, that too will be remembered. All of these things, and a hundred others, can tip the balance and induce a well-meaning school employee to call the child welfare system. Or perhaps it is your mother or a neighbour who calls the authorities after an argument.

You might be investigated, and the case closed, but you now have a file. Perhaps they want to help you. They recommend parenting classes, but you miss a few because of your shifts or because you could not find an adult friend to stay with your kids. Or you live in a neighbourhood with poor public transportation. Or you do not like the facilitator, who seems to know little about the world in which you live, or you bring a bit of attitude because you believe yourself to be a good mother, or you are just too tired to go. That doesn't look good.

Or, perhaps you do neglect or abuse your child. Most of us cringe when we remember some of the things we have or have not done while raising our children, and we hope they forgive us. For most of us, their forgiveness is all that is required, but for a mother on income assistance who has come to the attention of the authorities, many more questions are asked. Do you smoke when your children are at home? Do you use drugs? Drink? Where do you get the money for cigarettes and alcohol? Is there food in the fridge? Are you feeding your kids properly? Are you reporting your income accurately to the authorities each month? At this point, two systems might come into play. You will be asked to provide additional information to the welfare authorities and, if you ignore or postpone responses, your already-inadequate income might be reduced or delayed.

Suppose the worst happens, and your children are taken into care. The authorities are committed to reuniting families, so they will give you a series of tasks to perform to improve your parenting skills. Your children might visit you if there are volunteers to provide rides. If not, visits might be cancelled with no notice even though you may have re-scheduled shifts to be available. Or you can visit your children — if you can arrange time off work and a ride. If your children are confused by the situation and cry, you might feel bad and decide not to visit the following week. That is a mistake; it shows inadequate commitment on your part. And your attitude is important; if you have the wrong attitude, people will draw conclusions about your parenting skills. Then there are other implications. When your children are in care, your income assistance is reduced, and your Canada Child Benefit stops. Of course, this is only reasonable because foster parents are taking on the financial burden of raising your children. Except that when your income falls, you can no longer afford your apartment, which makes it more difficult to demonstrate that you could care adequately for your children if they were returned. The income assistance provided to single adults is pitifully inadequate. A temporary care order can quickly escalate.

Mothers who rely on income assistance do not have the luxury of being bad parents or even having a really bad week. There are bad parents in all income classes, and every parent has been a bad parent at some point, but most of us are insulated from relentless supervision because we have a secure, adequate and predictable income. Money is power, and not just for the plutocrats who run the world. An adequate, secure income is an almost inconceivable source of power for a poor mother.

Basic Income and the Multiplicity of Female Experiences

Basic income will not change gender norms overnight. It will not eliminate family violence (although it might provide the means for a woman to leave an unhappy marriage). It will not even, in itself, encourage more men to take on unpaid caregiving tasks, at least not as long as enough women are still prepared to do them. Some women still fare badly enough in the labour market that taking an unpaid sabbatical to do something else seems a reasonable option. On the other hand, basic income will also not cause mass female flight from the paid job market. Basic income will, however, provide many Canadian women with a secure, adequate and predictable income that is not subject to the discretion of caseworkers. This simple change will empower women (and men) in ways that are almost unimaginable to those of us who have adequate resources.

If there is a single takeaway message, it is that not all women are white, highly paid professionals for whom the price of housing in Toronto or Vancouver and the cost of daycare are the most pressing concerns they face. For these privileged women, any gap in work history will have lifelong consequences in terms of earnings, pensions and career advancement. There is no question that these women work hard, struggle with work-life balance and probably daydream about not having to work. They are certain that daycare subsidies are a more important expenditure than basic income, largely because they can see how it would improve their lives. They imagine that a basic income will create an incentive for similar women to leave the workforce, and they worry about losing the progress that women have made. However, the reality is that basic income will be irrelevant to such women. If they are single, they will not leave behind a high salary to live on $17,000 a year; if they have a partner, it is almost certain that their family income will be too high for them to qualify anyway.

The only women for whom basic income may create an incentive to leave the labour market are the low-waged. Some will be better off financially not working than they would be working, especially when they take childcare into consideration. How is the world better off if a woman pays someone else to care for her children while she struggles at a low-paid job? Staying home for a few years with young children will not have an appreciable impact on the lifetime earnings, pensions or career progress of low-waged women. Low-waged, insecure work will always exist, and when unskilled women re-enter the workforce after their children grow up, they will not be worse off than if they had continued to work. A few years more or less experience will not change the probability of significant career progress.

A basic income will not undermine women or reverse the gains that we have made in recent years. However, the poor and marginalized women who have not shared the labour market gains we celebrate will gain a great deal. A basic income is good for women.

Chapter 7
How Basic Income Affects Different People

Government programs affect different people in different ways. While all of us will benefit from the existence of a basic income program that reduces the risk of income insecurity, there are particular issues that are important to some groups. Some people face higher-than-usual risks of low income: people with disabilities, women, Indigenous people, single mothers, people aged forty-five through sixty-four who live alone, young people and recent immigrants. As a consequence, these groups of people will benefit from any program that effectively reduces poverty. Basic income, however, may have additional effects for some of these groups that should be carefully considered.

Basic income redistributes income. It can offset, at least in part, the financial consequences of social inequality, but it cannot address, on its own, the deep divisions that persist in our society. Basic income will not eliminate systemic injustices like racism or sexism, nor is it reasonable to expect it to. It will not reverse a legacy of colonialism experienced by Indigenous people. Basic income does not prevent or excuse anyone from working toward greater equity. It does, however, make the lives of those living with the consequences of systemic inequities more bearable as we work to address the underlying issues.

It goes without saying that no one is just a person with a disability, or just a newcomer to Canada or just a woman. Every one of us wears many labels, some more apparent than others. Racialized women face different stresses and opportunities than do white women; and Indigenous men with mobility challenges who live in remote communities face different challenges than do newcomers to Canada with invisible disabilities. Basic income will benefit every one of us in different ways. For some of us, its advantages will be much more immediate; for others, it represents a sense of safety that lives at the back of our mind and gives us the courage to take a risk. For some of us, basic income raises particular issues that we need to think about before the policy rolls out system wide.

Indigenous People

Almost 5 per cent of the Canadian population identifies as Indigenous — Métis, First Nations, non-Status or Inuit. Indigenous people in Canada have a low-income rate of 23.6 per cent, compared to 13.8 per cent for non-Indigenous people.[1] The poverty rate for Indigenous children is 30.4 per cent — twice as high as for non-Indigenous children. The average total income of an Indigenous Canadian was 75 per cent that of a non-Indigenous person in 2015. The average total income for a First Nations person was $31,519 — 66 per cent of that received by a non-Indigenous person.[2] On the basis of the numbers alone, Indigenous people, and especially First Nations people, stand to gain from a basic income because they are more likely to be living in poverty.

For Indigenous people living off reserves, the consequences of a basic income will be much the same as they are for other Canadians. Basic income will provide insurance against income insecurity, and provide a few extra dollars for those living on low incomes. It will provide a cushion to allow people to think about training for new jobs or to start new businesses. However, Indigenous Canadians, particularly First Nations and those without status living on reserves or in remote communities, might experience basic income differently than other Canadians. Many First Nations communities are in rural and remote locations. One of the consequences of isolation is that necessary goods, like food, are often only available at great expense because of shipping costs. Heating and household maintenance are very expensive due to the extreme weather of many locations. Transportation, particularly transportation to major urban centres, is often simply unavailable. Rural bus service is extremely limited in most parts of the country and, for many locations, roads might not exist. Northern airfares on scheduled routes cost much more than urban Canadians pay to travel to Asia or Australia, and airports are often far from where people live, which adds to the cost of a trip to the city.

The cost of living in isolated parts of Canada makes clear one characteristic of a basic income program: basic income alone cannot solve all issues related to poverty. Basic income relies on the premise that individuals can buy the goods and services they want to buy, but a cheque from the government will not help a great deal when markets do not exist or do not work well. Food security in the far north will not be ensured by giving local residents the same basic income that someone in Scarborough receives then directing them to a market that charges twenty-five dollars for four litres of milk — if it is available at all. Housing security will not be ensured when there is no rental market for housing. This is an issue that we face with all universal programs in Canada. It would be extremely complex and not particularly effective to adjust national programs like the Old Age Security pension and the Canada Child Benefit to take account of regional costs of living. Nor should we adjust the basic income. More reasonably, we could recognize that the very small proportion of Canadians (both Indigenous and non-Indigenous) living in remote conditions require additional support through other policies and programs along with a basic income.

Many First Nations people live on reserves, but not necessarily in remote locations. There are also special considerations that policymakers need to consider with respect to on-reserve First Nations. It is easy to imagine that a regular inflow of income to individuals living on a reserve might make a difference in terms of individual and social well-being and might also be a source of support for fledgling start-ups just as it would be off a reserve. A basic income would also be portable; a First Nations person who moves to a city would still receive the benefit. Currently, the movement of people between First Nations communities and the city often results in gaps in coverage, although some provinces are working harder than others to co-ordinate systems. Many people living on reserves do not complete income tax forms because they have no taxable income. Sometimes, though, the decision of on-reserve residents to not complete tax forms is more than error and oversight; in some cases, it is a political protest against a history of colonialism. As a consequence, they do not receive many refundable tax credits (such as the Canada Child Benefit) to which they are entitled. If a basic income were to be delivered through the income tax system, effort would be required to address this issue among First Nations people as well as other people who do not complete tax forms for whatever reason.

The largest problem, though, even for non-isolated reserves, is that many Indigenous communities lack the infrastructure that we take for granted in high-income industrialized nations. A basic income cannot substitute for access to clean water and decent wastewater arrangements. A basic income will do little to ensure access to education if the local school is closed because of structural or health issues. Access to health care will be limited, even in non-remote locations, if public transportation to larger cities is inadequate, and residents must rely on medical referrals with restricted access. A basic income will only work if it is built on the infrastructure that most people not living on reserves or in isolated Indigenous communities take for granted: the existence of clean water, access to health care, public transportation, and functioning markets that can provide access to affordable rental housing and good-quality food at prices comparable to those paid elsewhere in the country. A basic income in a community without this foundation will still be useful to residents, but it would be much more effective with infrastructure policies in place.

In the wake of the Truth and Reconciliation Commission, we cannot contemplate the implementation of a basic income without consulting First Nations, Inuit and Métis leaders. Local decisions about how to live in community might encourage local leadership to advocate for communal rather than individual control of resources, or some combination of the two. In either case, a basic income should not be a substitute for other programs designed to deliver needed housing, health care, education and food security to First Nations.

One issue that might be relevant to the discussion is the justification for a basic income. This book has treated basic income as a simple income redistribution policy, and no attempt to justify it has been made beyond the desire to reduce income insecurity. However, basic income can be thought of as a dividend payable to residents for the use of the original resources of the territory. These resources have resulted in economic growth that has benefited some people more than others. Alaska's Permanent Fund Dividend, for example, pays all residents an annual dividend funded by the revenue from oil sales.[3] This is an interesting model with obvious relevance for Canada's Indigenous population.

People living in Indigenous communities — whether these are urban reserves or remote Inuit communities — have a different relationship with the federal government than other Canadians. Indigenous people have their own sovereign authorities. Consultation with these authorities will be no less, and no more, complex than negotiations between provinces and the federal government, or negotiations required for any other national policy. Basic income offers an opportunity to test our commitment to the hard work of real reconciliation.

Racialized People

People who identify as non-white in Canada have, on average, lower incomes than do white Canadians, and this population is growing. In 2016, non-white Canadians made up 22.7 per cent of the population and received, on average, incomes that were 74 per cent of those received by white Canadians, a number that has remained virtually unchanged over the past decade. The low-income rate among non-white Canadians was 20.8 per cent, compared with 12.2 per cent for white Canadians.[4] It is easy to be unaware of the different ways that people of different races or ethnicities experience life in Canada because so few of our systems are set up to record race. For example, the data compiled by our health administration systems does not routinely include data on race. This has led some of us to complacency — a belief that if we think race doesn't matter, then it doesn't. With the exception of new immigrants, who might face a period of hardship as they settle in, or perhaps Indigenous people, who have faced generations of bad policy, we like to think that all other Canadians have equal access to the opportunities they need to succeed.

Race, like gender, remains an important barrier to economic well-being. Because Canadians of colour are, on average, more likely to earn low incomes, face job precarity and suffer from poverty, they will also benefit disproportionately from a basic income. Basic income cannot address the fundamental challenges posed by race and ethnicity in Canada, but it can offset some of the economic consequences.

Young People at the Beginning of Their Working Lives

Many young people remain financially and emotionally dependent on their parents well into their twenties. Decisions to stay in school longer and delay marriage and parenthood have changed popular perceptions of when adolescence ends, and adulthood begins. Some experts have argued that changing the definition of adolescence to include those up to twenty-four years of age might lead to more "developmentally appropriate" framing of laws, social policies and systems.[5]

Like every other group of people, youth aged eighteen through twenty-four are not homogeneous. Some are fully independent, supporting themselves in the workplace. Others are on their own and not faring nearly so well. Youth experiencing poverty have different developmental needs than adults. They are learning to be independent and often take more risks than adults. They are less likely to make use of formal services, and often rely instead on the informal help of friends and acquaintances. They are vulnerable to exploitation and often have significant government involvement in their lives. Almost half of homeless youth, for example, have recently left the child welfare system. Young people who turn eighteen with few skills, no resources and no parents to fall back on do require a program to alleviate poverty and help ease their transition into adulthood. It is not clear whether an unconditional program such as a basic income or a program with some constraints and conditions better meets the needs of these young people.

Youth just entering the labour market have little work experience and do not generally command high wages. This is, for most people, a temporary situation. A thoughtful and mature young person might choose to use a basic income to supplement earned income while working to gain experience, becoming involved in education or even traveling to learn something about the world and about him- or herself. This basic income would also give a young person the opportunity to choose among employment opportunities to ensure that the work they take on will actually contribute to their skills and pay off over time. In a sense, what a basic income can do for young people is to level the playing field; many people from middle- and high-income families have always had the opportunity to work part-time or in low-paid jobs or to take on volunteer tasks to build their résumés while relying on their parents to subsidize them. Some choose to combine work with education or travel. Most parents who subsidize these activities for their own children believe they will pay off in the longer run, and it is reasonable to assume that other young people could also benefit from similar opportunities.

However, as many parents and most teachers will attest, not all young people are mature enough to make good decisions. Some will use their unstructured time to engage in negative activities while others will simply spend their time doing very little at all. Gaining self-knowledge and experience, through work or travel or volunteer activities, can pay off in the long run in terms of better employability and higher wages, but long periods of time without useful engagement can have negative consequences. This is known as labour scarring. Young people who leave a job quickly forget the specific skills they might have learned with previous employers as well as general skills associated with working for a living, and the effects can persist far into adulthood. This deterioration of skills is associated with lower employability and lower wages over the long run. The negative effects are compounded if future employers perceive periods of unemployment at a young age to be indicators of lower productivity or poor work habits, or if the psychological effects of youth unemployment affect confidence and people skills. Unemployment in youth that is not offset with training or other educational activities is associated with lower wages and bouts of unemployment in adulthood.[6]

Basic income is based on the assumption that adults can and should make their own decisions and must abide by the consequences of those decisions. Yet, we also know that some people of all ages can make very poor decisions if they are given the freedom to do so. Adults who harm no one but themselves should be free to make their own decisions without the oversight of a committee of experts who believe they know better. This is the fundamental advantage of a basic income over existing income-assistance programs in which caseworkers can intervene to "help" adults who do not want to be helped. The freedom to make bad decisions, however, is usually limited to adults.

Determining the age at which a reasonable majority of people show the capacity to make rational decisions is something that a well-designed experiment could help us do. It would be very useful for at least one of the high-income jurisdictions planning ambitious basic income experiments in 2018 to focus some of its time and resources on this particularly vulnerable group. The answer is important for several reasons. The costs associated with a basic income for this age group are a significant portion of total costs; young people earn less than adults for many reasons. Political support for a basic income program is likely to wane if too many adolescents playing video games in their parents' basements receive a cheque. Most importantly, young people will benefit most from a support program designed specifically to meet their developmental needs. For this particular group, support may well require conditions such as job search, or hours contributed to education, training or approved volunteer activity. An experiment could help us determine the optimal design.

Newcomers to Canada

In 2016, there were 1.2 million immigrants (3.5 per cent of the total Canadian population) who had arrived within the previous five years. Their low-income rate was 31.4 per cent, and the average total income of a recent immigrant was 63 per cent that of a non-immigrant.[7] Should newcomers to Canada be eligible to receive a basic income?

Accidents of history and geography allow Canada to have reasonably good control over its borders. Recent increases in refugee claimants who arrive through non-traditional channels have attracted a lot of attention, but the numbers are small enough that we can easily absorb these newcomers along with regular immigrants and refugees and, as our history has shown us, benefit from the energy and productivity they bring to Canada over the long run. Few Canadians see newcomers as a threat to the feasibility of basic income. Offering newcomers enough to live on while they establish themselves is a good investment.

People with Disabilities

Many people live with physical or mental impairments, but a disability is an impairment that is not accommodated by the surrounding environment, making it more difficult for someone to perform daily activities. Impairment only becomes a disability when a person's social and physical environment does not meet their needs. Past studies have consistently shown that people with disabilities are less likely to be employed or to have a university education; they have lower median incomes overall and are more likely to live in low income.[8] A Statistics Canada study found that approximately 20 per cent of the population aged twenty-five through sixty-four lived with a disability in 2014, and of these, 23 per cent were in low income, compared with 9 per cent of those without a disability. The low-income rate varied by disability type, with those suffering both mental-cognitive and physical impairments most likely to be affected. People with a disability aged forty-five to sixty-four who lived alone and single parents with a disability accounted for nearly a quarter of the total low-income population in 2014.[9]

Quebec announced a basic income program to begin in 2018 for people with a severely limited capacity to work. In 2010, a study by the Caledon Institute of Social Policy called for a basic income plan for Canadians with severe disabilities.[10] In some ways, it is easier to contemplate a basic income for people who are not expected to work, and fewer than half of Canadians with disabilities are employed at all. A basic income would address poverty among a group of Canadians at particularly high risk. Yet some of the most vocal criticism against the Ontario basic income experiment related to its potential effects on people with disabilities.

Some people with disabilities face additional costs associated with their disability.[11] These costs fall into two categories: specific costs and general costs. Specific additional costs are for pharmaceuticals and adaptive devices such as wheelchairs and hearing aids. Arrangements differ by province, but these are normally paid for by provincial insurance for those people who receive provincial disability support. General additional costs are non-specific costs that are not covered and vary dramatically between individuals. For example, the additional rent that might be required for an apartment with an elevator or close to shops and services is a cost that is not covered by any existing program. To address specific costs for people with disabilities, Ontario offered extended health care insurance to people with disabilities who participated in the basic income experiment as it had previously done for people who received Ontario Disability Support (ODSP). General additional costs were accommodated by offering basic income recipients with documented disabilities an additional five hundred dollars a month. Since most people with disabilities face no additional general costs while a few face extremely debilitating costs, the five-hundred-dollar amount seems somewhat arbitrary.

Ontario might have followed a different path. Programs to cover specific costs associated with a disability might be opened to all Ontarians on the basis of the level of their income, so that working people earning exactly the same annual income as someone receiving ODSP would receive exactly the same support. Co-payments would increase as other sources of income increase. This change would eliminate the welfare wall that currently exists for ODSP recipients and is perpetuated by the Ontario basic income design.

> I would like to say that the program is called "Ontario
> Disability SUPPORT Program." What support do I receive?
> The best thing I can say about it is that it pays for most of my
> drugs. Without that support, my family would be beyond
> broke. — Amanda

General disability-related costs are more difficult to assess. For many people, there are none. For a very few, the costs are prohibitive. For this very small proportion of the population with heavy needs, some provincial capacity must exist to assess needs and to devise a personalized support. It is futile to try to attach an additional "disability payment" to a basic income in hope that it will meet all needs.

A basic income will, however, meet the needs of most people with disabilities. If the basic income program made no distinction between people with disabilities and those without, there would be an additional benefit. No one would have to qualify for support beyond demonstrating financial need.

> I am 34 years old and I have epilepsy. Kira is my seizure
> response dog. I was finally approved for ODSP. How low do
> you want a person to feel? It is a system that needs to change.
> They dig really deep into your personal life to see if you

qualify, and then review it as if your disability is going to go away. I receive $928 a month, which includes an allowance of $78 for my service dog. — Amanda

The documentation of disability is not simple. Impairments exist along a spectrum, but under existing programs, a decision must be made about when an impairment becomes a disability and therefore eligible for support. An individual applying for support must present documentation from a medical practitioner who is asked to provide medical data and to document the extent to which the impairment interferes with the activities of daily living and the applicant's ability to work or attend school. Often, the outcome depends as much on the skill of the clinician at completing forms as on any objective assessment of disability. It is not unusual to apply several times before succeeding. This process creates two sets of casualties: Those who are ultimately successful, like Amanda, read the clinical assessment and walk away convinced that their future will be bleak. Those who are not successful often find themselves ineligible for support and yet unable to find and hold a job. These are often people suffering from mental-health and invisible disabilities.

The Ontario experiment was also criticized for the decision to eliminate case management for basic income recipients with disabilities. One of the most debilitating fictions about income assistance and disability support is that recipients are incapable of planning, incapable of making good decisions and incapable of caring for themselves without the assistance of caseworkers. In some instances, the most important benefit of a caseworker is to work through a maze of confusing regulations and bureaucratic dysfunction that ought not to exist in the first place. That is, the poor design of the income-assistance or disability-support program itself generates the need for a caseworker.

I have had issues with ODSP in different ways.

First off I have had about three or four caseworkers and this was not by choice, they just bumped me to someone else without telling me.

I bring in my forms, appointment cards, cover letter, list of transportation and my form they give me to fill out and get them date stamped. Excuse my language but I can't tell you the number of times because it was happening so frequently the shitload of letters I got saying they didn't receive my forms! I started calling with copies of the info I have and stated back to them "well I have a copy date stamped from the office saying that the papers were delivered on — and I personally handed them in so I know they were delivered."

I have also been on the Rent-Geared-to-Income Housing list for twelve years. I understand that everyone needs a place to live and right now I have that with my parents. However, not being able to live on my own does in a way deprive me of a chance at independence.

ODSP does cover medical things. However, they don't tell you everything that is covered so unless you set up a meeting with your caseworker you might not know that orthotics are covered. We only found that out by overhearing someone at the desk and somewhere on the form it asks if you are on ODSP.

I think having a caseworker may be a good thing in the long run, I just wish it was consistent and that they gave you a solid list of medical benefits and coverage in a hard copy so that you aren't searching for hours to find an answer. You can only search so far on their website. Mom only knows some stuff by being part of an online ODSP support group. — Amanda

Would a basic income that offered clearer entitlements and fewer opportunities for discretionary decision making still require caseworkers to provide "wraparound care" for everyone — whether they wanted it or not? One of the best reasons for undertaking a basic income experiment is to gather evidence about the decision-making capacity of ordinary people. Time and again, given the opportunity, recipients make decisions that address the needs they consider most pressing.

People with disabilities will benefit from a basic income, as long as a system is in place to assess the special needs of the very small group of people who face prohibitive costs associated with their disability. Most programs can manage special cases and catastrophic costs. It is unreasonable to imagine that a basic income program could not.

Race, Age, Ability and Basic Income

One of the fundamental benefits of basic income is that it respects individual differences. People can use their access to a basic income to meet their own needs and those of their families as they see fit; they need not rely on government bureaucrats to discern and address their particular needs. As different as each individual and family is, however, there are some experiences that affect those of particular races, genders or ages in unique ways.

When we examine the data by race, age and ability, we see both why we need a basic income in Canada and how basic income needs to be developed in the context of other social policies. Basic income will not reverse racial discrimination, nor will it reverse the gains made in recent decades through changing social attitudes and the policies that reflect these changes. Basic income cannot offset the astronomical food prices, broken water delivery systems and non-existent housing on First Nations reserves, nor will it bring roads to isolated northern communities. Basic income will not ensure that foreign experience and credentials are fairly considered by the Canadian labour market, nor will it equalize opportunities for racialized Canadians. In all these cases, however, it will make the lives of recipients of all races and genders a little easier, reduce the poverty rate and ease the fears of those living with insecure incomes. It will bring choice and self-respect to many people who have been scrambling. Basic income is not an invitation to ignore the profound rifts in our society, but it is an opportunity to improve the well-being of many.

Basic income will have different impacts by age. Single adults between forty-five and sixty-four — people who now experience the greatest depth of poverty in Canada — will therefore benefit disproportionately. Young people also face considerable poverty in Canada. Those aging out of the care system and those striving to establish themselves in an inhospitable labour market, as well as many children under eighteen who have left home because they found their family life intolerable, certainly require support. A basic income would get money into their hands. But is an unconditional basic income the best way to deal with youthful poverty? Young people make up the only group of Canadians who might be better off with a more directed program — the equivalent of a much-expanded Canada Workers Benefit, for example — that would provide more structure to the lives of young people in need and direct financial support to those engaged in approved activities such as work, job training, education or approved volunteer activities. This call for engagement is driven by new discoveries in psychology that suggest many young people may not be ready to make decisions with long-term consequences at the age of eighteen. We desperately need data on how a basic income (and its alternatives) would affect young people.

Several jurisdictions around the world have undertaken basic income experiments of different designs, and others have pledged support for feasibility studies. Not one has identified young people as a population of particular concern and tested basic income and alternative policies (along with existing policies) for this age group. This is a missed opportunity of gargantuan proportions.

Chapter 8
Nine Myths About Basic Income

Any significant change in social policy raises concerns among the people who would be directly affected by it, among those who expect their taxes to pay for it, and among those who have an interest in existing programs that might be affected or even eliminated by the change. All of these disparate interests and competing groups share one fundamental characteristic: they believe that any potential gain from change is not worth even the smallest risk of loss. These fears underlie several myths about basic income.

MYTH #1
A basic income is just a covert attack on the social welfare system.

Advocates for basic income like to point out that it is one of the few programs that has friends across the political spectrum, with Conservatives as likely to support the concept as those who vote for the NDP or Green Party. They are less likely to point out that it also has critics across the political spectrum. Basic income is a policy that can take different shapes. It can be a generous addition to a social safety net that includes medicare, public education and other social supports. It can also be proposed as a stripped-down system in which recipients receive cash instead of all other support and are expected to go into the market to buy the goods and services they require. Like any other social program, basic income can be properly designed and funded, or it can be badly designed and underfunded.

Critics of basic income fear loss and therefore draw our attention to the fact that Milton Friedman, who has never been seen as a supporter of big government or generous income assistance, was an early advocate of basic income.[1] More recently, the support of the Fraser Institute has taken a similar direction.[2]

A stripped-down and underfunded basic income is not the system basic income advocates in Canada envision, it is not the system introduced in Quebec, and it is not the system that was piloted in Ontario. Basic income, in Ontario's pilot program, was seen as a substitute for income assistance and therefore a substitute for Ontario Works and the income-assistance portion of the Ontario Disability Support Program. Everything else stayed in place. Public education and health insurance were not under attack, and no one proposed that labour legislation be abandoned. Employment Insurance and the Canada Pension Plan, both federal programs, serve specific purposes such as support during spells of temporary unemployment and insurance-based retirement and disability support. They, too, stayed in place. The Canada Child Benefit and OAS/GIS are basic income-like programs for families with dependent children and seniors, and they were also retained. Basic income substituted for provincially delivered adult assistance and became part of an articulated social welfare system rather than a substitute for it. And, in fact, the Ontario basic income experiment was proposed in a political environment in which other supports, such as daycare, labour legislation and pharmaceutical benefits were being expanded rather than retrenched.

Adult benefits in most provinces are comprised of general monetary assistance as well as a set of direct benefits, such as extended health care, which includes things like dental care and pharmaceuticals, shelter allowances and such items as the "Special Diet Allowance" that can be prescribed by a physician in support of individuals with conditions such as diabetes who require fruits and vegetables that are an expensive part of the food budget. These programs also come equipped with case managers.

The decision about which of these programs to maintain and which to replace with a monetary equivalent is not an easy one, but there are principles to guide policymakers. Programs, such as extended health care, that can be shown to be more efficient and effective if delivered publicly should stay in place. The reason this program should be delivered publicly is because the benefits are not equally required across the population. A small number of individuals use a very large portion of the benefits because they have complex health conditions. Delivering such programs publicly means that a particular expenditure can be allocated to the people who need it, and low-cost individuals can subsidize high-cost individuals. Other goods, such as the Special Diet Allowance, work differently. Everyone needs to eat, and all of us, not just people with diabetes or other conditions, require healthy food. Everyone, therefore, should have the capacity to buy a healthy diet, and there is no good reason to have a separate program with different eligibility and oversight requirements to manage it. This is the height of inefficiency. Such programs should be turned into their monetary equivalents and added to basic income. If basic income were to be rolled out generally across the population, the obvious response would be to offer programs such as extended health care either universally or on the basis of the level of family income rather than its source. It makes little sense to subsidize the pharmaceutical needs of a recipient of income assistance but not those of a working individual who earns exactly the same income.

REALITY CHECK: Basic income in Canada is one policy among many rather than a way to replace all existing social programs.

MYTH #2
Eventually, governments will want to cut back on expenditure. It is better to keep an inefficient, complex, uncoordinated and bureau-

cratic system in place because it will be harder for a government to control.

If income assistance and disability support payments are replaced by a basic income, there is no guarantee that a future government will not reduce the basic income. Unfortunately, that is true of all social programs, including the existing ones. Over the past thirty years, cash entitlements to income assistance have declined in real terms, and individuals have increasingly been forced to access support in the form of food banks, school breakfast and lunch programs and other directed, usually stigmatized, benefits. In Ontario, for example, the value of income assistance for a single person in 1992 (in 2013 dollars) was $12,273 while it was only $8,224 in 2013.[3] The basic income is an opportunity to reverse that trend and to return dignity to families.

REALITY CHECK: The complexity of the current system has not prevented cutbacks. Badly designed and bureaucratic systems waste taxpayer dollars that could be redirected to recipients. In any case, there is something distasteful about a system predicated on confusing elected representatives.

MYTH #3

A basic income requires less bureaucracy, which means that a lot of good administrative jobs will disappear. In some small communities, these are the only good jobs.

If provincial income assistance were replaced by a basic income, fewer people would be required to enforce the onerous regulations of the existing system. However, there would still be a requirement for some administration. A basic income is not entirely mechanical; it must be able to respond to emergency situations, and this requires administrators. If, however, some people are no longer required to enforce existing regulations, there is an opportunity to redeploy highly educated and highly engaged labour into useful tasks that could actually benefit clients. People become caseworkers and social workers because they want to help their clients; most would prefer not to spend so much time trying to interpret baroque regulations to ensure that their clients have enough to survive, and most are not happy with a system that expects them to ensure their clients comply with all the regulations of the system. Both clients and caseworkers would be happier if they could partner to meet the real needs of their clients.

REALITY CHECK: It is always better for everyone to employ labour in useful tasks than to waste it.

MYTH #4
A basic income is just a wage subsidy. It will benefit employers because they will be able to pay workers who receive a basic income less, but workers will be no better off.

In Canada, we have a wage subsidy program called the Canada Workers Benefit (formerly the Working Income Tax Benefit), which is modelled on a similar program in the United States called the Earned Income Tax Credit. To receive benefits under these programs, an individual must work and receive a wage. The wage is then subsidized by the program. Up to a certain income level, every dollar earned results in an increase in benefits. Someone who does not work receives nothing. This kind of a program puts all the power in the hands of the employer. Potential workers only receive benefits if they work, so they will accept almost any work, at whatever wage is offered, to survive.

A basic income works differently. It is not a wage subsidy; it is not tied to the hourly wage rate or dependent on employment. No one will be desperate to take any job offered at any wage because they will receive the basic income whether they work or not. If the position is degrading or the wage insufficient, they can refuse a job offer. No one is required to work to survive. A potential employee has the power to walk away.

Mincome offers some evidence to support the claim that, if anything, a basic income will raise wages. David Calnitsky digitized employer sur-

veys that were completed by Dauphin business owners during the Mincome project and by business owners in some similar towns in which
workers were not eligible for a basic income. The Dauphin business
owners claimed that they were forced to raise wages in Dauphin after
the introduction of Mincome because (in the words of one disgruntled
respondent): "[Mincome is] just spoiling people rotten and upsetting
the workforce something unreal. The hours people have to work, the
wages they get, and the output they give (which isn't much) just make
it impossible for the average employer to even stand a chance at hiring
help."[4] Mincome, at least in the view of some local employers, gave
workers far too much power because it allowed them to reject low-paid
or poor-quality jobs and to demand higher wages.[5]

The argument that any improvement to social security is an alternative to higher wages is an old one, but there is little evidence to support
it. For example, a proposal that Canadian families should have access to
a family allowance paid to mothers was debated in Parliament as early
as 1929.[6] This proposal was opposed on the right by groups such as the
Social Services Council that argued family allowance undermined the
principles of marriage because it would be paid to mothers rather than
fathers. On the left, it attracted the opposition of the Canadian Trades
and Labour Congress, forerunner of the Canadian Labour Congress,
which argued family allowance would act as a wage subsidy and suppress wages. Family Allowance was not introduced in 1929, and as a
consequence, Canadian families had no access to this financial support
through the lean years of the 1930s — the longest stretch of real wage
decline in Canadian history. Family allowance was again debated after
World War II. It was supported by the Co-operative Commonwealth
Federation, forerunner of the NDP, in 1942, and opposed again by the
Canadian Trades and Labour Congress on the grounds that it would
be an alternative to a general increase in wages. The Canadian Trades
and Labour Congress argument convinced the Department of Finance,
which worried about wage inflation after the war. The Department
of Finance supported the introduction of family allowance hoping

that it would, in fact, limit wage growth just as the unions predicted. The family allowance was consequently adopted in Canada just as the most sustained period of real wage growth began. Far from suppressing wages, it accompanied a real wage increase. The *Family Allowance Act* was the keynote of the 1944–45 parliamentary session and was described by one advocate as "the most radical, expensive, unlikely and popular legislation of the 1944 postwar program."[7]

Anyone convinced by the argument that basic income will suppress wages can take solace from the fact that we do have labour legislation and minimum wage laws in Canada. A basic income does not do away with the need for regulation.

REALITY CHECK: Basic income is not a wage subsidy, and it will neither reduce wages nor slow wage increases. It will reduce coercion of low-waged workers, who will have the opportunity to walk away from poor job offers. If anything, basic income might put pressure on low-wage employers to improve the terms and conditions of work.

MYTH #5
A basic income will reduce the number of people working low-wage jobs, and we need someone to do that work.

A basic income will give workers the ability to walk away from jobs they consider poorly paid or demeaning. Employers might raise wages (which also entails raising prices) to attract workers. If consumers are not prepared to pay higher prices, either the firm will go out of business, it will produce abroad with lower-priced labour, or it will automate. Automation is a growing possibility in many industries, but the trend toward automation has been underway for a long time. In 1964, most tomatoes in California were picked by low-waged migrant workers. President Lyndon Johnson was concerned that competition from these workers was driving down wages for Americans and responded by making it more difficult to hire migrant workers. By 1966, 94 per cent of the tomatoes in California were harvested mechanically.[8]

Many low-wage jobs are in the service sector and, specifically, in the restaurant industry. Franchise owners complain that they cannot pay higher wages because consumers will not pay more for the food they serve. These jobs cannot be done abroad, but some of them can be automated. If the jobs cannot be automated, and consumers are unwilling to pay enough to staff the restaurant, then we will have to do without the cheap food such places serve. This is the same issue that faces low-wage employers when the minimum wage increases.

Some people take this argument one step further. They note that some of the biggest consumers of fast food, for example, are low-income people. Therefore, they argue, raising minimum wages or introducing a basic income hurts low-income people the most. We should, however, recognize that low incomes and low prices are connected. We can continue to operate the low-price, low-wage, low-income economy we have been chasing in recent years, or we can recognize that it is possible to extract ourselves from this vicious cycle and pay decent wages even in the restaurant industry, as do many European countries. Higher prices allow the payment of higher wages. It is unfair to force low-waged workers to bear the disproportionate burden of poverty.

REALITY CHECK: Some low-wage jobs might be lost because workers have the freedom to reject the work. If employers will not, or cannot, increase wages, they will shift production abroad, automate or shut down. A basic income will help displaced labour adjust.

MYTH #6
A basic income will just shift bad jobs abroad, and we should do our own dirty work.

Some might argue that a basic income in Canada will have the effect of shifting the lowest-paying and most unpleasant jobs abroad. Indeed, one of the consequences of higher-priced labour in Canada is that some employers will look for alternatives, either in the form of automation or by shifting production to a lower-wage region. This trend has characterized production in high-wage countries for almost fifty years. When local labour becomes "too expensive," producers shift production abroad. Many people look at the conditions associated with textile production in Bangladesh, for example, or electronics factories in China, and question the morality of sending our most indecent work abroad for others to do. This is not the fault of Canadian labour legislation or "privileged" workers in high-income countries, but rather the result of consumers in high-income countries who choose to purchase products produced by exploited labour. Nevertheless, there are two quite disparate views about the extent to which workers in low-income countries suffer because high-income countries shift their least pleasant and lowest-paying work abroad.

The standard economic argument claims that everyone benefits from trade. Workers in low-income countries benefit from the additional work created by our demand for the low-priced products created in conditions that we would not impose on workers in our own country. As long as foreign workers are not coerced to work under exploitative conditions, as slaves and children might be, for example, the assumption is that they have freely consented and presumably benefit from the decision or they would not take the job. The freedom to leave such work acts as insurance; the alternative opportunities available to such workers must be less pleasant than the jobs they accept. Therefore, as bad as the conditions may be, foreign workers benefit in the sense that they are better off than they would be without this additional opportunity. And, in fact, there is some evidence to support that perspective. In recent years, Chinese workers have become "too expensive" for much of the work that we used to export to China, and the work is instead sent on to even lower-wage South Asian countries. That is, the increased demand for Chinese workers to produce products for the North American market put upward pressure on Chinese wages and improved their working conditions.

While these workers are worse off than workers in high-income countries, they are better off than they used to be. In turn, it is claimed, South Asian workers will soon benefit from production for the North

American and European markets, and their wages and working conditions will improve. However, it is hard to accept this argument when we read of textile factories that lock their workers inside and hide child employees when foreign inspectors arrive.

An alternative view asks whether lack of coercion is sufficient to ensure that labour is free to consent. Workers are not free to consent to work at indecent jobs when the only other opportunities open to them will not feed their families or allow them to live with a modest degree of self-respect. If they do not have the capacity to live decent lives without working under exploitative and degrading conditions, we cannot claim that they are benefiting from the work we send abroad. However, the solution is not to force Canadian workers to accept lower wages or inappropriate working conditions so that Canadian consumers still benefit from low-priced consumption goods. The solution is to work for improved labour conditions abroad, to put binding restrictions on the use of temporary foreign workers in Canada and to advocate among Canadian consumers to ensure that our consumption dollars do not support labour exploitation either abroad or at home. If Canadian consumers continue to buy cheap goods produced abroad, then they are encouraging such conditions by default and have effectively decided that the working conditions of foreign labour are not their concern. In any case, it is both unfair and ineffective to try to improve the conditions of foreign workers by forcing low-waged Canadian workers to work at these jobs by depriving them of a basic income.

REALITY CHECK: A Canadian basic income might result in some of the lowest-paid and least-pleasant Canadian jobs moving abroad. If we are concerned about the conditions of labour in other countries, the solution is to advocate among Canadian consumers to ensure that our consumption dollars do not support exploitation rather than to deprive Canadian workers of a basic income.

MYTH #7

A basic income will just raise prices.

Most of us have had the experience of watching low-rent housing become more expensive when shelter rates associated with income assistance increase. The result is that the government pays more but rents for the lowest-quality housing rise proportionately; no one benefits but the landlords. However, basic income is different from a shelter allowance or any other increase in income assistance provided for a specific purpose. Basic income provides unrestricted cash to recipients, and individual families will use that money to purchase different goods and services according to their needs and tastes.

From the perspective of Toronto or Vancouver, it might seem obvious that housing is the greatest need, and that any additional income will immediately be dedicated to improving the housing families have. As a consequence, all families will try to rent better apartments and landlords will capitalize on the increased demand and raise rents. However, even in Toronto and Vancouver, families have different needs. Low-waged working people who receive basic income might decide that better daycare is their primary need and allocate their extra money accordingly. Others will be satisfied with the housing they have and decide to spend a bit more on a better diet, or to buy new clothing or bicycles for their children. Others live outside high-rent jurisdictions; rents are much lower in Thunder Bay and Lindsay than they are in Hamilton or Toronto, and any attempt on the part of a single landlord to raise rent in response to an increase in basic income is likely to fail because there are other landlords and other apartments for low-income individuals. Additionally, landlords are limited in their ability to raise rents if rent controls exist.

It is possible to imagine that there might be particular instances where prices increase — at a local restaurant in a low-income neighbourhood, for example. If customers suddenly have more money to spend on modest luxuries, the restaurant might raise prices. There will, however, be no general increase in all prices when a basic income is introduced.

REALITY CHECK: There will be no general increase in the price level associated with a basic income although some local prices might rise in the short run when low-income people suddenly have more money to spend.

MYTH #8

A basic income is not a good way to reduce poverty. We need programs directed to the root cause of poverty that address the complex needs of homeless people with mental health and substance abuse issues.

The root cause of poverty for most people who would receive a basic income is a lack of money. More than half the people who would benefit from a basic income are working but not earning enough money to raise themselves and their families out of poverty. Most of the rest are single parents of young children. Even among the minority who are adults living alone, most are not homeless. A very small proportion of people who would be eligible for basic income support are homeless people with complex mental health and substance abuse issues. Just to put the numbers in perspective, it has been estimated that approximately 235,000 people in Canada experience some form of homelessness each year, and only a small proportion of these represent the core homeless with complex needs who are targeted by such programs as Housing First, a program that offers very significant supports to clients, providing them with permanent and stable housing, supportive services and connections to the community-based supports people need to keep their housing and avoid returning to homelessness.[9] By contrast, the Parliamentary Budget Office estimates that more than 7.5 million people would benefit from a basic income if the Ontario plan were rolled out nationally.[10] The vast majority of people who would receive support from a basic income do not require intensive support services. They simply require enough money to meet their needs.

There is, however, a need to think more clearly about homeless people with complex needs. Housing First, which is an excellent model for addressing their needs, comes into their lives after they have spiralled out of control. Its purpose is to reduce demand for services such as emergency department care in hospitals, police interventions and similar services that are very heavily used by a very small number of people with significant issues. Most people, however, are not born homeless, addicted and mentally ill. When people end up on the streets, it is usually because of a series of bad breaks, often coupled with poor decisions. Marriages end, businesses collapse, young people leave unhappy homes and people overuse alcohol and drugs to avoid the reality in which they find themselves. Substance abuse leads to evictions, and a lack of money makes it difficult to find new housing. Homelessness is a barrier to even menial jobs, and unemployment exacerbates poverty and deprivation. Homelessness makes any existing mental illness or substance abuse issue harder to deal with. Social isolation makes all these problems worse. Housing First intervenes at this point to try to help people recover. What if they had access to enough money to support their basic needs before their lives became so desperate?

Most basic income recipients are not homeless people with substance abuse and mental health issues. However, even people vulnerable to substance abuse and mental illness might avoid worse outcomes if they had access to an adequate basic income before they became homeless. Having enough to eat and a roof over your head makes it easier to access the other services you require. That is, after all, the philosophy behind Housing First.

REALITY CHECK: Most people who would receive a basic income are not homeless people with substance abuse and mental health issues. The vast majority are currently living as well as they can given the resources available to them. Basic income will simply make their lives a bit easier and reduce the financial risks that might lead to homelessness. The very visible, but nonetheless small, proportion of people who are homeless and have complex mental health needs require additional supports.

MYTH #9
We can get better results with less risk by building on the programs we already have in place.

Many of the benefits of a basic income occur because a family has a more adequate, predictable and secure income than they had previously. Consequently, health improves, and children do better at school. Families feel less stigmatized and are more able to fully participate in the community. If we put the same amount of money required for a basic income into existing programs, however, we will not see the same effects.

Can we expand income assistance and disability support instead?

Families who receive income assistance will welcome higher incomes and will benefit. However, an expansion of income assistance does nothing for working Canadians whose incomes are too low to allow them to escape poverty. Therefore, the health and educational benefits to be expected from a basic income will not be realized if the financing is directed instead to income assistance.

Moreover, design flaws in income assistance cannot be eliminated within the current structure. The bureaucracy and administrative inefficiency of provincial income assistance exists because the programs are governed by too many rules. The rules were put in place to ensure that those who can work look for jobs, and that only those who have no other resources available to them receive support.

Paradoxically, these difficulties are also in place and are even more onerous for people with disabilities. People with disabilities receive higher income support under the existing scheme than do individuals who receive income support from the general scheme. Disability support programs, which vary by province, typically consist of several components, some of which are designed to assist individuals seeking employment or education or to provide particular forms of personal assistance or medical devices.

The existing programs, which require individuals to qualify on both

financial and medical grounds, create substantial barriers for qualifica-
tion. It is particularly difficult to document mental health conditions, and
whether one is approved often relies more on the diligence of the professional completing the form than on the nature of the condition. Individuals who do qualify are asked to reappear at a future date, so that program
staff can determine whether the medical condition has changed. There are
also periodic reviews during which recipients are asked to meet with a caseworker. The system is emotionally draining even for those who qualify.

Qualifying for disability support is challenging, and the outcome is
unpredictable. Additional supports may or may not be available, depending on the discretion of caseworkers. As is the case with general income
assistance, caseworkers are charged with simultaneously advocating for
their clients and policing recipients to ensure that no fraud occurs.

The bottom line is that expanding a broken system by investing more
money in it will not fix its structural problems.

Can we expand the GST Credit, the Canada Workers Benefit and related provincial programs instead?

While basic income has been seen in Canada as a replacement for
income assistance, there are other programs that could be expanded
instead. One possibility is the set of federal and provincial refundable
tax credits that supplement earned income. This has the advantage
of addressing the needs of low-waged workers, and it simultaneously
satisfies those taxpayers who fear that a basic income will encourage
people to work less.

This policy has been implemented across most high-income countries
to a greater or lesser extent. The United States has, for many years, been
eliminating cash entitlement programs and replacing them with various
forms of earned income tax credits and other forms of workfare. The
Organisation for Economic Co-operation and Development has, for
decades, supported these "active labour market policies."[11] These programs focus on shifting government spending away from income assistance that has no work requirement to programs with work and training

requirements, and reforming tax and benefit systems to remove work disincentive effects and make work pay.[12] These policies have, however, never been consistently applied across countries. Some have put work requirements in place but not enforced them while other countries have been much more focused on ensuring that recipients actively worked or searched for work. One significant limitation became clear during the recession of 2008: these policies do little to help people when there are no jobs to be had. The economic theory behind creating work incentives is very clear and convincing, but there does not seem to be strong evidence that they actually work very well.[13] As a consequence, there has been a general shift away from heavy-handed workfare programs.

In the United States, the trend in many states has been to ask for more in exchange for aid. Time limits, asset tests and work, training or volunteer requirements have been added to the Supplemental Nutrition Assistance Program (food stamps), as was done in the 1990s with Temporary Aid to Needy Families — a program which is still frozen at the same level of funding. The results are ambiguous at best. Work requirements in the United States largely coincided with a period of economic growth, so many people did move off welfare rolls, and the poverty rate did decline. The question is whether these individuals would have done so anyway — without the work requirement. And while the individuals and families that have succeeded are doing better financially, those who are left behind are the most vulnerable, and they are subsisting on less and less support. People with disabilities, particularly those with invisible disabilities who cannot qualify for disability support, people with addictions or criminal records and those who live in areas with limited job opportunities and no public transportation find the requirements difficult to meet.[14]

Without doubt, an expanded Canada Workers Benefit is better for low-waged workers than no program at all.[15] It remains an open question whether it actually encourages more people to work. In the same way that a basic income probably encourages a small number of people to work less, an expanded Workers Benefit will probably encourage a small number of people to work more. In Canada, the very modest size of the program limits

its usefulness. However, a wage subsidy cannot meet the needs of the most vulnerable: people with barriers that prevent them from working need unconditional income assistance best met through a basic income.

Can we use minimum wage and labour legislation to address poverty instead?

Strong labour legislation and minimum wages are a complement to basic income, but not a substitute for it. Everyone, especially the low waged, benefits from strong labour legislation. However, it cannot be a substitute for basic income for the simplest of reasons: most poor families have no one working at minimum-wage (or near-minimum-wage) jobs, and many of those working minimum wage jobs do not live in poor families.

Workers nineteen or younger are much more likely to work for minimum wage than anyone else, with the next highest incidence of minimum wage among those aged twenty through twenty-four.

In 2016, almost half of fifteen- to nineteen-year-olds worked for minimum wage as did 15 per cent of those twenty through twenty-four. While the growth rates of older workers working at minimum wage

Table 8.1   Share of Employees Working at Minimum Wage (or Less) By Age, Canada and Provinces, 2006 and 2016

	Total, 15 years and over		15–24 years		15–19 years	
	2006	2016	2006	2016	2006	2016
Canada	4.4	6.9	16.1	26.5	31.3	49.1
Newfoundland	7.6	5.9	26.2	19.7	38.5	35.3
Prince Edward Island	4.6	8.2	1.8	3.1	1.4	1.9
Nova Scotia	5.9	6.6	21.6	23.7	37.2	44.1
New Brunswick	4.2	6.6	14.7	26.2	29.9	50.9
Quebec	4.2	6.1	15.7	24.9	31.0	44.7
Ontario	4.8	9.2	20.1	26.7	41.1	69.9
Manitoba	4.8	6.8	16.3	22.7	29.5	35.6
Saskatchewan	5.5	3.5	17.9	12.3	31.9	24.1
Alberta	1.7	4.5	5.1	15.5	9.4	27.6
British Columbia	4.7	4.8	14.4	15.7	26.0	30.5

Source: Armine Yalnizyan, "Why a $15 Minimum Wage Is Good for Business," *Macleans*, June 2, 2017.

are dramatic, only 3 per cent of prime-age workers and 4.3 per cent of those over fifty-five are working for minimum wage. Many others, of course, will be working at wages just slightly higher than minimum wage. Without denying the real hardship of low-waged work, one of the reasons the incidence of minimum-wage work has increased in recent years is because legislated minimum wages have been increasing more quickly than mean hourly wages. This has led to a compression of wages at the low end. People who used to earn just slightly more than minimum wage did not receive wage increases when the legislation changed.

A minimum-wage increase, then, will increase the incomes of some adults and some low-income families. However, using increases in the minimum-wage rate as a lever to reduce the incidence of poverty is, at best, extremely inefficient. If employment declines at all in response to wage increases, some of those previously earning minimum wage will no longer be employed. Even if we set aside any negative impact on employment, an increase in the minimum wage will increase the disposable incomes of many people who do not live in low-income families. Two adolescents will benefit for every adult woman who gains from a wage increase, and four young people aged fifteen through nineteen will take home larger salaries for every adult male who benefits. While

20–24 years		25–54 years		55 years and over	
2006	2016	2000	2016	2000	2016
6.7	15.1	1.7	3.1	2.5	4.3
19.2	11.7	4.4	3.3	5.3	5.0
7.6	19.0	1.6	3.7	2.6	4.7
12.1	13.8	2.6	3.4	3.1	4.4
5.1	10.9	1.8	3.0	3.3	5.0
6.9	15.5	1.8	2.5	2.9	4.0
7.1	20.3	1.6	4.0	2.0	5.0
6.6	15.6	1.8	3.7	3.3	3.3
7.2	5.9	1.9	1.5	4.0	2.6
2.2	9.2	0.8	2.3	1.0	3.1
7.5	8.3	2.2	2.4	3.7	3.5

higher incomes are, no doubt, appreciated by teenagers, and while some teenagers live in low-income families and contribute to total family income, it is much more efficient to target assistance directly toward low-income families than to increase the wages of all low-income workers and hope that some of that largesse will increase total income in low-income families.

Isn't it better to offer a jobs guarantee?

The idea behind a jobs guarantee is that the government should either subsidize business or act as an employer of last resort, to ensure that the economy operates at full employment, and that everyone who wants to work has the opportunity to do so. Everyone would therefore contribute to society as a worker and would gain the self-respect and positive benefits associated with independence and hard work.

While this proposal sounds good and has attracted a lot of attention over the years, governments have not generally proven themselves capable of creating decent jobs for everyone. Therefore, in practice, this means that the government will subsidize private sector employers to create more minimum wage jobs for low-skilled workers who are generally the most vulnerable to involuntary unemployment. Low-skilled workers who earned near minimum wage before the jobs guarantee will soon find themselves competing with subsidized workers to keep their jobs. This will have the effect of shifting much of the cost of low-wage labour from private firms to the government. While wages cannot fall below minimum wage, the increased competition from new workers at the bottom of the wage scale will not encourage firms to raise wages, even for those workers earning slightly more than minimum wage.

A jobs guarantee creates monitoring costs in addition to the direct subsidy. If assistance depends on work, administrators are required to ensure that individuals are linked with available jobs, appear at job interviews, accept job offers and perform the jobs for which they are hired. Others must monitor the various labour markets to ensure that subsidies are sufficient to ensure full employment. Still others are required to ensure that those firms receiving subsidies actually create the new jobs they promise to create. This is an expensive proposition, and its administrative costs would far exceed traditional income assistance programs.

There is, however, a further problem. Whenever traditional income assistance programs are reduced, or time limits are placed on assistance, the disability lists in the same jurisdictions swell. A jobs guarantee would not apply to people "incapable" of working; there would be exceptions for the "genuinely" disabled. The difficulty is that there is no clear distinction between people with disabilities and those without. There is always a grey zone in which milder barriers to work exist. Whether an individual with such disabilities is designated disabled depends on whether that individual seeks disability status, and whether he or she can convince a practitioner to support the designation. In a jurisdiction in which being disabled is a condition of receiving support, it is only reasonable to expect that more people would seek disability status, and more practitioners would support disability designations for people with milder barriers to work. Guaranteed jobs will have the perverse effects of increasing monitoring costs, acting as a drag on market wages and reducing the size of the labour force by causing disability rosters to soar.

Why don't we just reverse the neo-liberal decisions that have created job insecurity?

In the 1950s and 1960s, good unionized jobs in manufacturing were available to people without college degrees. These jobs paid family wages, so that one working adult could support a family in middle-class comfort: houses and cars were bought, and children were sent to university. Since then, decades of changes in the labour market have undermined this system. Freer trade has opened manufacturing in high-income countries to competition from low-wage economies. More significantly, automation has replaced many of the routine tasks that these workers performed. Displaced workers found new jobs, but the new work was in non-unionized sectors such as professional services and retail trade, and the features of this work made labour organization less successful. Even within industries, the nature of jobs changed, and newly created jobs were less likely to be unionized. Private sector unionization rates began their long downward path. As the nature of work continues to change, and competition becomes international in scope, labour organization becomes even more difficult.

Even when the unionization rate was at its peak, however, there were limitations to its coverage. Those who belonged to a union received good health insurance, a decent pension, guaranteed severance pay and other benefits. Those who did not belong to a union had little insurance against economic insecurity. As a consequence, there was pressure on the government to step in and provide many of these benefits: we now have universal health insurance, government pensions including the Canada Pension Plan, legislated parental leaves and other benefits for all workers.

The decline in unionization rates occurred during a period when the public sector stepped back and attempted to de-regulate private firms, cut corporate tax rates and encourage entrepreneurship to stimulate economic growth. Firms facing labour shortages received a sympathetic hearing from governments and expanded the use of temporary foreign workers — guest workers with no real path toward citizenship who were prepared to work for wages that Canadians rejected.

While many of these specific changes can be and are being challenged, there really is no way to turn back the clock to 1955. Automation will continue to expand and displace unskilled workers. The public sector, which has resisted some of these changes more successfully than the private sector, can only expand so far. Service industries, particularly those that are international in scope and accessed via online platforms, do not lend themselves to shop stewards and old-fashioned labour organization. The demand for platform workers will, however, continue to grow, partly because it is difficult for any jurisdiction to tax international firms that organize in these ways. These firms generate very high profits for their shareholders at the expense of benefits for their workers. At the same time, the expansion of government programs has reduced the relative benefit of union membership by providing many of the benefits that unions used to provide for their members.

REALITY CHECK: A basic income will allow Canadian families to live with dignity as the economy and the jobs it produces evolve. It will reduce the depth and breadth of poverty while simultaneously addressing the design flaws of existing programs that allow too many to fall through the cracks. Neither putting more money into existing programs, nor redesigning these programs by tinkering at the edges nor wishing to turn back the clock on economic change will yield similar results.

Chapter 9
Can We Afford a Basic Income?

Basic income has been debated for decades in Canada and for centuries around the world, but for most of that period, there has been little agreement on the best design. The one bedrock point of agreement is that basic income should not depend on behaviour; people who qualify should have a right to income to meet their needs without demonstrating that they have searched for work or attended programs to make them more employable. Beyond that, plans have varied dramatically. How much money should people get, and should it be given to everyone or targeted to low-income people? If it is targeted, how quickly should it be clawed back as income rises? What existing programs should it replace? The cost of the program to taxpayers can vary dramatically depending on how these questions are answered.

Until very recently, the lack of agreement about the details of design has made it difficult for advocates to answer a question most people care about: how much is this going to cost taxpayers? Some critics have offered ridiculously high estimates in the hundreds of billions of dollars annually. In the last few years, however, there has been a convergence on many of the details of how a basic income in Canada should look. While there remain a few people who argue that basic income should not be targeted but rather given universally to rich and poor alike, their voices are increasingly being drowned out by those who believe that the Canada Child Benefit offers a good, feasible and affordable design that can be adapted for working-age adults. Similarly, while a small number of people continue to suggest that all existing social programs could be replaced by a basic income, most people view basic income as one aspect of social policy, designed to deliver monetary support to low-income people better than the existing mélange of provincial and federal programs, but in no way adequate to replace such fundamental aspects of the social safety net as public health insurance, public education or even programs targeted to specific groups of people with high needs, such as people with profound disabilities or substance abuse issues.

The details are still open for discussion. How high should the guarantee be? Should income be calculated on an individual or a family basis? How much income should recipients be permitted to earn tax-free before the benefit is reduced? How quickly should the benefit be reduced as income increases? Nevertheless, the big issues are settled: basic income, in Canada, is targeted to low-income people on the basis of need. It is universal in the same sense that health insurance in Canada is universal: we do not all use it equally, but the program is there for us when we need it. Basic income, in Canada, is not conditional on work effort; it is not a subsidy for low-waged jobs, and it does not depend on the discretion of caseworkers to make decisions about how to enforce a complex set of regulations. Basic income, in Canada, trusts individuals and families to make decisions in their own best interests.

The Cost of a National Program Modelled on the Ontario Experiment

A recent study by the Parliamentary Budget Office — the independent and non-partisan office that provides analyses of the state of the nation's finances — has cut through some of the confusion about costs. Conservative Member of Parliament Pierre Poilievre asked a simple question: "If the Ontario scheme were to be rolled out across the country, how much would it cost?" Since Ontario had to make decisions about design elements to implement its pilot, the Parliamentary Budget Office had something concrete to work with.[1]

If every Canadian between eighteen and sixty-four were offered a basic income of $16,989 ($24,027 for couples), less 50 per cent of earned income, and if disabled people received an additional $6,000 per year, the gross cost to the federal budget would be a staggering $76 billion per year. However, the federal government currently spends $32.9 billion to support low-income Canadians in this age group. If the money the federal government currently spends on refundable and non-refundable tax credits and special programs for low-income Canadians of working age were spent instead on a basic income, the federal government would only have to find $43.1 billion to pay for a national basic income.

This is still a great deal of money. However, the Ontario pilot was set up as a potential alternative to Ontario Works and the Ontario Disability Support Program — basic income assistance for working age people with and without disabilities. In Ontario, these programs cost eight billion dollars each year, and if we assume there are similar costs in other provinces, that represents an additional twenty billion dollars, not including the costs of administration.[2] If it were possible to reallocate this provincial expenditure to a national basic income, a challenging task we will consider in the next chapter, the net cost of a national basic income would fall to $23 billion. A net cost of $23 billion is starting to look decidedly less utopian. In fact, the Canada Child Benefit costs that much every year.[3] None of this takes into account any potential savings on the administration of provincial income assistance, which is simply not knowable from current data sources.

However, basic income should be seen as an investment rather than a cost. While the fundamental purpose of introducing a basic income is to allow all Canadians to live modest but decent lives whatever economic challenges they face, there is a hard-edged economic rationale for addressing poverty: the consequences of poverty are expensive. In the Mincome experiment, hospitalizations fell by 8.5 per cent among basic income recipients relative to a group of similar people who acted as a control group; in 2017, Canada spent more than $67 billion on hospitals alone. There were similar reductions in visits to family doctors. I didn't have the data to examine the impact on other social programs, but it's not hard to imagine that other costs are also driven up by poverty. A basic income is one way to slow the relentless increases in the costs of other social programs that enter peoples' lives after poverty has left its mark. Some advocates argue that savings on social programs will be greater than the costs of the program.[4]

Current Federal Government Expenditures and Revenues

To put the net costs of a basic income into perspective, it helps to know how much the federal government pays out each year and how much it receives in tax revenue. If we were to roll out the Ontario program nationally, it would cost an additional $23 billion beyond what the federal government currently spends, assuming the $20 billion currently spent by the provinces on income assistance can be recovered. That means that we would have to find some combination of programs to cut or taxes to increase to cover its immediate costs even if, in the long run, a Basic Income might end up saving us money on other social programs such as health care. But how does the federal government currently spend its money?

In 2016–17, the federal government spent $311 billion.

Figure 9.1   Federal Government Expenditures, 2016–17 (billions of dollars)

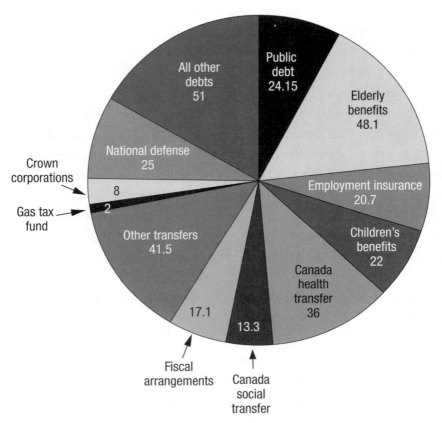

Source: Department of Finance

Since tax revenue pays for most of government expenditure, it helps to understand which taxes generate the revenue that the government of Canada relies on. In 2016–17, about half of government revenue came from income tax on individuals, just over 14% from corporation tax and almost 12% from the GST.

Figure 9.2   Federal Government Revenue, 2016–17

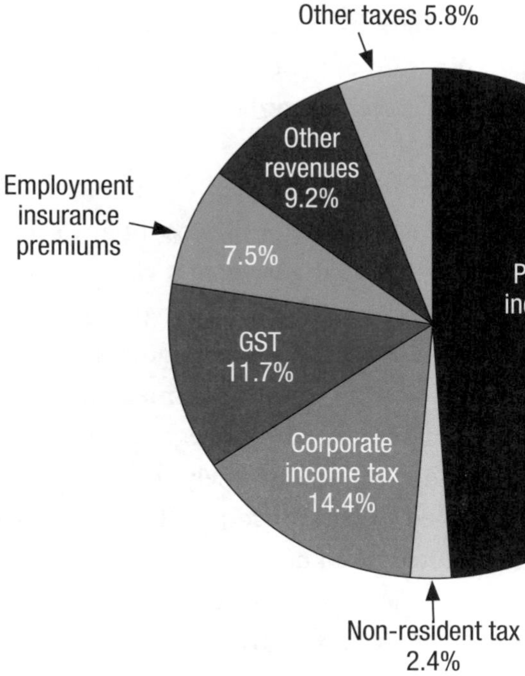

Other taxes 5.8%

Other revenues 9.2%

Employment insurance premiums 7.5%

GST 11.7%

Personal income tax 49%

Corporate income tax 14.4%

Non-resident tax 2.4%

Source: Department of Finance

Government expenditures were paid for through tax revenue, which is all ultimately paid by individual people, and by government borrowing. If expenditures exceed tax revenue, the government will finance the resulting deficit by borrowing, either from Canadians directly, from the Bank of Canada or from foreigners. The government deficit in 2016–17 was $17.8 billion. Any deficit in the current year will be added to the stock of debt which was created by borrowing in the past. The debt, in 2016–17, incurred interest payments of $24.15 billion. Unlike households, the federal government has no need to pay off the debt; the size of the federal government debt becomes a problem only when the government pays so much in interest payments on that debt that its ability to offer other programs is compromised.

If a new program such as Basic Income were to be introduced, there are only two sources of funding: either the government can reduce its expenditure on other social programs, or it can increase its tax revenue, or it can rely on some combination of the two. The costs of an ongoing program cannot be paid for by government borrowing.

How Behaviour Can Affect Costs

One of the limitations of trying to estimate the cost of any social program is that it is difficult to forecast the ways that human behaviour might change as a result of introducing the new program and the implications these changes will have for cost. Economists like to talk about "incentivizing" behaviour and typically assume that we respond far more than we really do to monetary advantages and disadvantages.[5] This is what accounts for some of the extremely high estimates that some economists have attached to basic income.[6] Their concern with behavioural change is overstated. We know most people working full time are unlikely to quit their jobs when offered a basic income of $17,000 annually, and most of us don't have the flexibility to decide how many hours we'd like to work each year. We work the hours we're asked to work. Many people are working part time when they would work full time if a job were open to them.

There is, however, a different kind of behavioural change that these critics point to: a basic income must be paid for by someone. This means that tax revenue will have to increase. There are a variety of ways to raise taxes, and each will have different effects on the economy. Critics focus on the potential impact of higher corporate taxes on business investment and of higher marginal tax rates on highly paid labour, arguing that not only will a basic income encourage the poor to work less, but it will also encourage firms to invest less in Canada. Professionals and other highly paid labour, they argue, will relocate to lower tax jurisdictions, particularly the United States. Again, this fear is dramatically overblown. There are many ways to increase taxes, most of which do not involve raising marginal tax rates, and the overall costs of the program can easily be absorbed.

The estimates of the Parliamentary Budget Office effectively undermine the claim of unaffordability. While $23 billion annually sounds like a tremendous amount of money, it is a very small proportion of total federal expenditure. Even if we choose to increase taxes to pay for the program, the benefits will surely be worth the additional costs. In the words of journalist Andrew Coyne: "Three points on the GST to end poverty? Guaranteed income sounds like a good deal."[7]

How to Design a Basic Income

The Ontario model is, of course, not the only way to set up a basic income. Several other people have estimated the annual cost of a basic income based on different assumptions about who would be covered by the program, which other programs it might replace, how high the guarantee would be and how quickly benefits would be taxed back. Some of these are summarized in the Appendix, and the important thing to notice is how much the estimates vary depending on the design decisions made by the author.

Every decision about how to design a basic income has important implications for cost, fairness and efficiency. There is no perfect design: each decision involves trade-offs. These decisions are based on value judgments rather than economics, so this is not a set of decisions to be left to experts. All Canadians have a stake in ensuring that our social policies reflect our collective values. Consequently, everyone needs to be engaged in a public conversation about fairness, the importance of work and self-sufficiency, how generous we want to be to people who have different values than we do, and how prepared we are to give the victims of bad luck or bad choices a second chance. And how will we translate that collective decision into social policy?

These are some of the decisions that we need to talk about:

How high should the guarantee be?

The trade-off is obvious: the higher the guarantee, the more the program will cost. Moreover, the higher the guarantee, the more likely some people will be to decide not to work at all.

How quickly should the benefit decline as income increases?
The more quickly the benefit declines, the less expensive a basic income will be for taxpayers. However, if benefits decline quickly, people who work might decide that working an additional hour doesn't make sense for them. A part-time worker might choose not to look for full-time work, or people might work less overtime. If benefits decline quickly as income increases, fewer people will receive anything. The Canada Child Benefit is reduced at a very gradual rate; as a consequence, the program is expensive, but it benefits the majority of families. If many people benefit, the program often has more political support than a more targeted program.

What should the benefit unit be?
Should basic income be based on individual income or on family income? In Canada, we pay our income tax as individuals, so a family with one high-income earner will pay more in taxes than a family with an identical total income divided between two earners. However, most of our benefits in Canada are based on family income. The Canada Child Benefit, for example, is based on the incomes of both parents, and income assistance in all provinces is based on total family income. The Guaranteed Income Supplement received by a married or common-law senior couple is lower than the amount that would be received by two unrelated people.

It costs more for a single person to live on her own than it costs each of two people who can share some expenses. For example, a two-bedroom apartment does not usually cost twice as much as a one-bedroom apartment. Therefore, it might seem reasonable to choose a family as the benefit unit. But at a time when many couples do not officially marry, do we really want to hire an official to determine the nature of the relationship between people who live together? If we simply take recipients at their word, we risk establishing a system that encourages people to misrepresent their circumstances. A benefit based on family income is one of the design features that current income assistance recipients resent bitterly about the present system, and it is a characteristic flaw in many Canadian social programs. The Canada Child Benefit, despite its many excellent features, is based on family income, and some single mothers have had their benefits reduced or clawed back when they were not able to demonstrate to the satisfaction of the Canada Revenue Agency that they were single parents.

Family relationships vary widely between population groups, by age, and even between similar groups in different provinces. Some marriages are formally sanctioned and relatively stable; other relationships are more fluid. The 2016 census shows fewer couples choose to formally marry, and among those who do, first marriages generally occur at a later age than in the past. The decline in marriage rates does not mean that Canadians are no longer choosing committed, long-term relationships, but it does make it harder for authorities to determine the nature of the relationship between people who live together. If policies are based on a "family," then resources must be committed to policing personal relationships. This raises the cost of enforcing the policy and undermines one of the benefits of a basic income, which is that there should be no need for the government to intrude into personal decisions.

Choosing a benefit unit on the basis of whether it creates an incentive to marry or divorce may seem odd to anyone but an economist; most people seem to think such a personal decision would be made for other reasons. However, there is a historical reason to be sensitive to this issue. The negative income tax experiments that took place in the United States forty years ago foundered on precisely this issue. Early results seemed to suggest that recipient families in Seattle and Denver were more likely to divorce than were controls.[8] These results convinced some people that a basic income would discourage marriage, particularly among African American families. This led some early basic income advocates, such as Daniel Patrick Moynihan, to withdraw support because they believed that marriage was one of the best ways to reduce poverty among women and children.[9] A decade later, the data were re-analyzed, and the conclusion that recipients were more likely to divorce was called into question. However, by that time policy debate had already moved on to other issues, and basic income was not on the radar any longer.[10]

Who receives the money?

The choice of benefit unit is distinct from the question of who actually receives the money. When family allowances were first established in Canada, they were made payable to the mother because it was believed that the mother was more likely than the father to spend the money in ways that benefited the children. Some family benefits in Canada are now payable to the lower-income adult, which is an attempt to offset potential power differences within the family. Delivering support to the lower-paid adult gives that person the financial capacity to leave a potentially violent marriage without worrying about whether they can afford to feed their children or keep them out of a shelter. We can deliver the money to the lowest-paid adult however we define the benefit unit; these are separate issues.

What role does age play?

At what age should we become eligible for a basic income? Ontario had designed its basic income to fill the gap between the Canada Child Benefit and OAS/GIS, so the government set eligibility between eighteen and sixty-four. In fact, the payout level that was piloted in Ontario is similar to the payout recipients currently receive from Old Age Security and the Guaranteed Income Supplement when people reach age sixty-five. At the other end of the age distribution, however, some difficult questions remain.

Many young people are financially dependent on their parents in many ways. In fact, if we model the Ontario design and extend it across Canada, as much as one-third of the net costs of the basic income are required to support single adults between eighteen and twenty-four.[11] Not everyone in that age group is dependent on their parents, but including single adults living with their parents will raise the costs of a basic income significantly because this group includes many people working less than full time at low-paying jobs. Sometimes, this is a choice made to facilitate education, and often this situation is temporary. How much do we want to spend to reduce the breadth and depth of poverty among a population that, in some but not all cases, has access to parental support? If we disallow payments to single adults who live with their parents, many of these young people will simply move out. That does not mean that they will not remain financially dependent on their parents. If we extend support to all young people at age eighteen, can we be certain that the money will not cause harm? There is always the temptation for older people to assume that young people do not have the foresight to make good decisions.

As an alternative, we could set the qualifying age for a basic income at twenty-five, and this limitation would be relatively simple and non-intrusive to enforce. However, increasing the qualifying age also causes difficulty because there is real poverty among eighteen- to twenty-four-year-olds. Young people, including those transitioning out of foster care, homeless youth and young parents, certainly experience poverty and economic insecurity. Moreover, this is the particular age group that most often encounters low-quality, low-paying work.

It is not clear whether a basic income or a more directed program that makes a benefit conditional on participation in approved work or study programs is the optimal response for this age group. We simply do not know how young people will respond to a basic income, or what the long-term consequences of their decisions might be. The benefits of a more intrusive, conditional program specifically for youth might exceed the costs. It is unfortunate that as of 2018, none of the existing basic income experiments intend to investigate this issue.

How should basic income align with other social programs? Basic income is built on the idea that families know how to spend money better than do experts. There are, however, exceptions. Health care insurance is one such example. There is a lot of evidence that private health insurance leads to more inequitable, ineffective and expensive outcomes than public health insurance. Therefore, public health insurance should be retained. Special benefits tied to income assistance are particularly badly designed. If someone who receives income assistance receives a benefit such as pharmaceutical drug coverage, why should a working individual with the same total income be denied such support? These kinds of benefits, if retained, should be based on level of income rather than source of income.

The bigger question is which federal and provincial programs and tax credits ought to be replaced by a basic income. Employment Insurance serves an important purpose: it provides support during temporary layoffs. The Canada Pension Plan is a work-related public insurance plan that allows workers to save for retirement and insure against disability. It, too, serves a useful purpose. Moreover, it has obligations to workers who have already contributed. Other expenditures, such as the federal GST credit, might be more easily rolled into a basic income.

This careful design work requires policy expertise and knowledge of the costs and effectiveness of current expenditures. People who currently benefit from existing programs and tax credits will, understandably, object to restructuring, but the decisions need to be based on clear principles. It may be possible to restructure programs so that no one is made worse off with a basic income than they would be under the current scheme, but it is not easy. More likely, there will be winners and losers as with any policy change, so the principles on which the redesign is based must be transparent.

What is less controversial is that programs designed to address other issues, such as addictions and mental health challenges, will not be replaced by a basic income. Individuals who benefit from such programs will still require support even if their material needs are better met. Basic income gives people money; it is not designed to address more profound social and health issues although many of these issues are clearly made worse by poverty.

How should the money be paid?

Many single mothers complain that their Canada Child Benefit changes too slowly while their income assistance changes too much from month to month. The best way to deliver a basic income may require a modified provincial system that reconciles accounts over a three- or four-month period.

Some of the strongest support for basic income is associated with the belief that we can eliminate a lot of bureaucracy by paying a basic income through the income tax system. This idea is reinforced when we call a basic income a negative income tax. As anyone who has waited eight months to get a response to a simple adjustment can tell you, delivering basic incomes to vulnerable people may strain the current capacity of our income tax system.

Most of us complete our tax forms and reconcile our income tax once a year in April. If we get a refund, it arrives in one deposit soon after. If we receive a GST credit or Canada Child Benefit, it might be paid monthly or quarterly, but it will normally be based on the previous year's taxable income, just as the Guaranteed Income Supplement for seniors is based on the previous year's taxable income. For low-income Canadians, and particularly for those who work and receive sporadic incomes, this poses a big problem. There is some capacity in the tax system to adjust payments for tax credits like the Working Income Tax Benefit (now called the Canada Workers Benefit) and the Canada Child Benefit, so that they are based on current and anticipated income rather than past income. Similarly, the Guaranteed Income Supplement can reflect expected income. These adjustments, however, are not automatic; they require specific requests and take time.

Provincial income assistance is intended to be far more responsive to changing needs. Some recipients of income assistance will receive the same amount of money each month, but many will not. It is paid monthly or biweekly and reconciled monthly. That is, the amount paid this month will be adjusted to account for any penalties imposed and income earned during the month. This prevents clients from accumulating debts to the system and responds relatively rapidly to changing needs. However, people who rely on income assistance often complain that they do not know from month to month how much money they will receive from the program.

A basic income could be set up to introduce some much-needed financial stability into the lives of low-income people. A government payment that they know they will receive with certainty allows someone to plan their expenditures and to better deal with unexpected needs. For a low-waged working person, in particular, a predictable basic income that does not vary each month might be very useful. Wages can vary a lot from month to month, and it is possible that wage-earners will not know exactly how much they will earn until the cheque arrives. Hours of work may not be guaranteed. Wages might be paid into a bank account that is in overdraft and seized by the bank, or workers may receive less than they expected because their employer charges them for uniforms or other supplies. Wages might be withheld for a variety of reasons, some of them unexpected. By contrast, a fixed income paid by the government could be an important source of stability. However, if the government payment is also adjusted each month to account for volatile earnings, and especially if unexpected penalties are imposed on that income, any attempt to budget can be thrown into chaos.

As an alternative to an unresponsive tax system and a too-responsive income assistance payment system, we could deliver the basic income through a modified provincial system that reconciles accounts over a period of several months. During that period, other income might fluctuate, but the recipient would receive a stable government payment. Someone who earns more than expected in this period will not be treated as having incurred a debt that must be repaid. Rather, basic income would be reduced going forward. Between adjustments, everyone would know with certainty how much they would receive.

There must also be a robust capacity to deal with unexpected emergencies. For that reason, some of the administrative capacity associated with income assistance must be maintained at the provincial level even after a basic income is introduced. This requirement, however, should be much less than that entailed by the current system, in which every payment is recalculated each month.

Should there be an asset test?

The ability of people to participate in the economy depends on both their income and their wealth or assets. Some people have little wage income but hold significant wealth. This group might include seniors with small pensions and a lot of wealth tied up in housing. It might also include professionals, such as physicians, who incorporate and reinvest earnings in the corporation rather than taking them as income or dividends. We can set the rules to ensure that a basic income goes only to people we want to receive it, eliminating professionals for example, but sometimes it is difficult to determine the appropriate response.

Fairness would seem to suggest that a basic income should be reduced for people with assets as it is for people with higher incomes. It is, however, not quite so simple. Financial assets held outside registered accounts typically generate incomes that will reduce the basic income benefit just as if they were wage incomes. Should the capital that people hold also reduce basic income? What about RRSPs, RESPs and TFSAs, which offer special tax treatment, as well as retained earnings in businesses, and real assets, such as vehicles and real estate? This is a very difficult political issue for any government. Assets held in registered accounts such as RRSPs and TFSAs have special tax treatment because a social decision has been made to encourage long-term savings. RESPs encourage saving for education. Should an individual who benefits from a basic income not also have the opportunity to save for retirement or for a child's education?

> Until three years ago, I was a pharmaceutical sales rep. Most
> of my income was commissions and I did pretty good. My
> company didn't have a pension plan, but they matched
> contributions I made to my RRSP. I had retirement savings

and my house was paid for. I had some other savings — not
a lot, but I was comfortable. Then I lost my job when the
company was bought up, then I got sick. So, I'm fifty-three
and out of a job. No one is lining up to hire an old guy with
cancer when they can get some twenty-five-year old and pay
them a lot less.

I'm pretty lucky. Lots of guys in chemo have got nothing. But I
had money saved to retire when I'm sixty-five. It's not going to
last very long if I start running it down at fifty-three. I can sell
my house, but I've got to live somewhere. This job is all I've
ever done but deliver pizza when I was a kid. Who's going to
hire me? I'm either "over-qualified" or "just not competitive."
No one says "you're too old." — Karl

How should we accommodate real estate and other assets, such as
vehicles? Most income assistance programs have raised asset limits to
allow the ownership of (at least) modest vehicles, and few people are
forced out of the family home when they require income assistance.
How much is too much? Any jurisdiction that introduces a basic income
will have to grapple with very different opinions. What seems obvious
to some will seem far too generous to others.

I lived in Japan for twenty years, returned to Hamilton last
year, have sold my condo and am leaving again. I wasn't
expecting the level of unemployment, substance abuse and
poverty I have witnessed and experienced. Both my boyfriend
and I are around fifty with no dependents. I stopped looking
for a job after ten months. (I have been living off an equity
loan.) My boyfriend has a criminal record and is ashamed
to divulge this information. He collects less than $1000 from
ODSP, rents a room for $400/month and is surrounded by
drug users. He has cried to me a few times on the phone

because of hunger and his situation. I thought about making an anonymous call to the police about the drug users but where are they going to go? The jail is overcrowded and there aren't enough rehab spots. And what would they do after they got out? A guaranteed minimum income will help people worry less, gain confidence, pay for licenses or training etc. and stop feeling like society's discards. If Ontario chooses a city for a pilot program, I hope it is Hamilton.

On the other hand, money is already going to people who do not need it such as: my ex-friend who is sitting on $2 million in real estate and has been collecting "welfare" through her children for ten years because she doesn't "want a measly job for $40,000 a year." She receives family help, travels, dines at restaurants etc. Or, my nephew who makes $100,000 a year, took his family of five on two overseas vacations in one year, receives a small payment for his three children every month and asked to borrow $40 from me.

I don't agree that the programs in place now are helping the people who really need it. Giving money to the "haves" because the government believes they will buy more and stimulate the economy (and go further into debt), while others are starving, is bizarre and corrupt. It is not creating a fairer society it is creating animosity.

If a guaranteed minimum income is introduced, I hope assets, including principal residence and vehicles, are taken into consideration. — I. McInally

This is a challenging political issue, but it is important to allow people to save and invest. Savings protect people from unexpected changes in their circumstances. People with savings are less likely rely on credit cards or payday lenders and can borrow money on reasonable terms from banks and credit unions when they need it. Savings create economic security, which allows people to relocate for new job offers or to take risks with self-employment. However, any government will need to negotiate very different opinions about how much is too much.

Developing a Canadian Basic Income

These design challenges are significant, but they are also an opportunity for all Canadians to reflect on the kind of society that we want to build. Basic income is an idea that is now in the air. It is being talked about by denizens of Silicon Valley and in the offices of the World Bank, the International Labour Organization and the Organisation for Economic Co-operation and Development. The 2018 Human Rights Film Festival in Geneva highlighted a documentary on basic income. Experiments are underway in the Netherlands, Finland and Barcelona, as well as the United States, and are being planned in France and Scotland. The shortsighted cancellation of the Ontario experiment is a lost opportunity. Unconditional cash transfers have had remarkable results in low-income countries around the world. But every one of these instances takes the idea of basic income and makes it concrete by making very specific decisions about these design issues.

What decisions would best reflect Canadian values — our generosity, kindness and willingness to give people second chances and, at the same time, our resistance to those who would take advantage? What kind of a basic income is right for Canada?

Chapter 10
Getting From Here to There

Canada will introduce a basic income at some point in the not-too-distant future. Provincial budgets are fiscally unsustainable. Our unwillingness to address poverty relentlessly drives up the cost of delivering health care. Health care costs now account for over 50 per cent of provincial expenditure in many provinces and are only feasible because the federal government sends $38.6 billion to the provinces each year to pay for it. Provincial income assistance offers support that is too low to allow recipients to live healthy and dignified lives, and this increases the costs of other social programs that try to respond to the social effects of poverty. More and more Canadians face a changing labour market that challenges our ability to support our families and plan for the future. This affects the health and well-being of people who have never had to depend on income assistance in the past. No one in Canada can assume that we will never face an unexpected health event, family disruption or job loss. Any one of us might need financial support at some point in our lives, and a basic income provides insurance that the support will be there if and when we need it.

The Parliamentary Budget Office has demonstrated that we can afford a basic income similar to the one under examination in Ontario. The net costs are comparable to the amounts we have been willing to spend for other social programs, such as the Canada Child Benefit. If an increase in taxation is necessary, there are many options available to us that will not disrupt the economy or place an undue burden on taxpayers.

However, the transition to a basic income is not easy. Provinces, territories, First Nations and even municipalities share responsibility for income assistance with the federal government. Co-operation between governments is challenging. Taxpayers already feel burdened, and many will resist any further increase. We are not starting with a blank slate. There are currently programs in place that attempt to address the consequences of poverty, some of which might be changed fundamentally if a basic income is introduced. People who deliver existing programs, whether these are currently delivered through the provinces or by outside agencies, are understandably loyal to the programs they created. Even if we agree that basic income is a necessary improvement, how can we overcome the hurdles of introducing a new program?

The Big Bang: Introducing a Fully Developed Basic Income All at Once

If a basic income is to be effective, it needs to be predictable, not dependent on work or job search and large enough to support a family at a reasonable standard. It must be accompanied by a solid system of social supports, such as public health care and education, but it might replace other government spending aimed at addressing poverty among the same recipients. It is reasonable to develop a Canadian basic income for people of working age because children under eighteen and those over sixty-five already have access to a form of basic income through Canada Child Benefits or Old Age Security and the Guaranteed Income Supplement.

It is (barely) possible that all levels of government might enter into negotiations to replace the existing patchwork of income assistance programs across the country with a national basic income delivered co-operatively. This level of co-operation hasn't been seen often. All the various governments would have to agree on the level of the guarantee, the appropriate tax-back rate and how responsibility for delivery would be shared between the provinces and the federal government to ensure that there remains some ability to deal with unusual cases. And then there is Quebec. This might be the best outcome, but it is also the least likely.

Similarly, it is (barely) conceivable that one or more provinces might choose to rework their income assistance programs into a basic income. If it is to be effective, the payments offered must be larger than income assistance currently provides. A real basic income also includes income supplements for low-income working people. An already-strapped provincial government would face higher costs as it attempts to send more money to greater numbers of people every month. Most of the smaller provinces simply haven't the fiscal capacity to consider this at all; they already have lower income assistance payments, higher income taxes and fewer provincial tax credits than the larger provinces. Even the larger provinces will find this challenging.

There is also the problem of how very different rates of support would play out across the country when people are free to move between provinces. People choose where to live for a variety of reasons and not just on the basis of how generous income assistance payments are, but it would be unreasonable to assume no one would relocate to a province that offered better support. Can any provincial government risk being first?

The Gradual Approach: Introducing a Basic Income that Grows over Time

It is much more likely that basic income will emerge in Canada gradually. The federal government has the capacity to introduce some kind of a basic income for Canadians. Even without the money currently delivered through provincial income assistance, the Parliamentary Budget Office estimates a net cost of $43.1 billion for a national version of the Ontario plan. However, if the provinces are still running provincial income assistance programs, the federal government might decide to offer a smaller basic income to Canadians, relying on provinces to pick up the slack. Suppose the federal government decided to deliver a basic income at half the Ontario level. The costs would be substantially lower for the federal government than a full program, and they could negotiate with the provinces as they did with the Canada Child Benefit to ensure that provincial payments will not be reduced as a consequence. Since the provinces will continue to offer provincial income assistance, the federal government need not make income delivery flexible enough to deal with emergencies or varying needs from month to month. As in the case of the Canada Child Benefit, payments could be made on the basis of the previous year's income (which might be adjusted for documented changes in circumstances) and paid monthly or quarterly, and families could continue to rely on provincial support to meet their varying needs.

This type of modest federal basic income has limitations, but its benefits would far outweigh the costs. Some people would still have to deal with the punitive provincial income assistance programs that discourage work and undermine self-worth. The oppressive administrative costs of provincial income assistance would continue to burden taxpayers and recipients, and an opaque, costly and ineffective provincial system would continue to deliver a patchwork of support across the country. However, the basic income could be offered at very low administrative costs because it could be delivered through the income tax system. Recipients would have a stable income they could count on every month for a full year, no matter what else happened in their lives, but they would also have the flexibility of provincial income assistance to deal with unexpected changes in circumstances. Low-waged working people would receive greater support under this program than they do currently. This modest federal basic income would also be quite distinct in the minds of taxpayers from provincial income assistance, which might lead to greater acceptability.

Over time, the basic income can be regularly increased until it reaches a target level sufficient to meet basic needs. Our capacity to pay for a basic income will increase as the economy grows. The amount of tax revenue that the federal government has to spend will increase at least as quickly as economic growth.

One way to ensure that all Canadians receive an equitable share of economic growth is to peg increases in the basic income to the real per capita growth rate of the Canadian economy, even after basic income reaches its target level.[1] Between 1978, when the last Mincome cheque was mailed, and 2016, the Canadian economy grew by 127 per cent. The population grew by 50 per cent during that same period, but economic growth was high enough that every adult and child in Canada in 2016 could consume 63.5 per cent more than their counterparts in 1978. Of course, not everyone shared the riches. Wage growth stagnated for much of the period, and the incomes of the poorest 20 per cent of Canadians barely budged. However, economic growth made increased government expenditure feasible.

As the economy and federal government tax revenue grow, the basic income can grow proportionately. Provincial income assistance will become less and less important to meet the day-to-day costs of supporting a family. Over time, we might expect to see the provincial investments reallocated to the kinds of support programs provinces can deliver better than the federal government because they are more responsive to local conditions: specific job training, housing or support programs aimed at local needs and unique circumstances.

There is another, much less effective, way that a basic income might be introduced gradually, and in fact the federal government has been following this plan since the 1970s. Instead of introducing a small basic income for all adults, the government could choose to offer a basic income to select groups of Canadians. For example, the OAS/GIS was offered to seniors, and this was politically acceptable because no one expects seniors to support themselves by continuing to work. The Canada Child Benefit was offered to families with children under age eighteen, and this was politically acceptable because no one wants children to suffer because of their parents' decisions. In 2017, Quebec announced what it called a basic income to people with disabilities. Other provinces are watching with interest. This, too, will be politically acceptable because no one expects people with disabilities to necessarily be able to support themselves through work. The simplified system saves the province some administrative costs and offers some people who have qualified for disability support more money with fewer conditions.

One problem with this form of gradualism is that people of working age without disabilities become less and less likely to ever receive a basic income because those who we believe have the greatest needs have already been taken care of. The old, costly and demeaning provincial income assistance program is retained as the sole source of support for working-age people without children or disabilities. It becomes easier for provincial governments to cut these programs or to introduce even more punitive restrictions because "deserving" people already have access to other supports.

Overcoming Vested Interests

Any new policy will advantage some people and disadvantage others. Most of us fear losing what we already have more than we appreciate advantages that we hope to gain. Therefore, potential losers are always ready to complain while potential beneficiaries are cautious enough to wait and see whether the benefits they have been promised will actually materialize. In the case of basic income, the policy can be designed so that no one currently relying on existing income assistance programs will be worse off. That, however, does not mean that there is no one who suspects basic income will be worse than the current system.

The basic income experiments conducted during the 1970s demonstrate how easy it is for a good idea based on solid evidence to be shunted aside by interest groups. In the United States, the experiments were opposed by an informal and unstable, but nevertheless powerful, coalition made up of old-school Republicans who opposed any tax increases and all "entitlement" programs and "progressives" in the federal Department of Health, Education, and Welfare and the Department of Labor.

The opposition on the political right was expected. The opposition on the political left, however, was more of a surprise. Many of the people charged with overseeing the experiments were the same people who had built the existing welfare programs and were loyal to them. Some were incapable of imagining ways of delivering programs other than those that were currently in place, but more were simply committed to programs they believed to be essentially well designed but underfunded. Rather than embark on an untried basic income, they argued, it would be better to just increase the funding to existing programs.

This position, of course, underplays the flaws of existing income assistance programs. They are poorly designed programs not simply because they pay recipients too little, but because they are organized in ways that undermine individual autonomy. Caseworkers oversee families, partly to help them make better life decisions and partly to ensure that the taxpayer is protected. This puts caseworkers in an impossible position: how do you build trust with your clients when your loyalties are divided? The sheer mass of regulation means that recipients are almost always not in complete compliance; consequently, they are always subject to penalties that might or might not be imposed. People who have no experience with the income assistance system imagine that benefits are clear and well understood; in fact, many decisions are left to the discretion of frontline workers. All of this means that a recipient never knows how much they will receive, and when it will arrive. They are inundated with routine paperwork. Late compliance means another penalty or discretion denied. None of this supports autonomy or rational decision making. The solution is not just to "raise the rates" but to replace a fundamentally flawed template.

Opponents in the Department of Labour brought a different perspective to the experiments. Their opposition was based on two points.

First, they held a somewhat romantic attachment to the nobility and dignity of labour itself. Second, they believed that any improvement to social security was an implicit attack on the primacy of organized labour and, ultimately, the well-being of workers. Labour advocates were therefore very interested in the reaction of potential workers to the receipt of a basic income. Many looked at the results and declared that the modest reductions in hours worked were, in fact, unacceptably large. They believed that any reduction in work effort would be bad for the economy, bad for society and ultimately bad for workers themselves.

The more fundamental opposition from those in the Department of Labour was a variant on an argument that has often been raised when labour advocates are confronted with proposed improvements to social security. The argument is that improvements to social security act as a subsidy to low wages, which allows employers to resist wage increases. Opponents in the Department of Labour believed that a basic income would act as a drag on the labour market and undermine improvements in worker well-being that ought to be achieved through collective bargaining.

The third group of opponents in the 1970s was made up of people outside government involved in delivering very specific kinds of support to particular groups of people. Very often these were small-scale initiatives focused on the needs of a single neighbourhood or group of people, such as the homeless or people with substance abuse issues. These programs were often very effective for their recipients, but they required a lot of time and money to work well. They also addressed issues that were not shared by most low-income people. Advocates for such programs declared that their programs had proven successful, and the money being "wasted" on basic income should be reallocated to their programs because it was clear that basic income would not help their clients.

While well meaning, this opposition was based on the false belief that their clients were representative of those who would benefit from a basic income. While particular groups of low-income people might require specific supports well beyond basic income, most people who would benefit from a basic income — that is, most low-income people — do not require these supports. Some of the single-focus programs are simply not scalable. A program that requires dedicated workers delivering particular services to a well-defined group of recipients might be effective, but it cannot easily expand to address the needs of an entire population.

This kind of opposition still persists. If basic income is designed to replace provincial income assistance, it asks those who work within the current system to recognize its flaws. People who have worked hard to improve the system over time will have difficulty getting past the idea that all they need is more money to expand existing programs. Labour unions have played an important role in improving living standards over the past 150 years. Even though the private-sector unionization rate in Canada today is less than 15 per cent, it is hard for insiders to accept that the role of unions has fundamentally changed. Today, members are far more likely to be highly paid government and hospital workers than factory hands. New forms of employment, such as online platforms like TaskRabbit, Etsy or Amazon Mechanical Turk, resist labour organization. Well-meaning volunteers or underpaid workers in social services have devoted many hours and years of their lives to making life easier for low-income people. Any changes, they believe, should come from those working on the front lines. Who are these outsiders who want to disrupt everything by introducing a basic income?

As basic income becomes better understood, some of this opposition might naturally fade. There will still be a role for government employees who work within the existing system; imagine the benefits for both the worker and the client if a caseworker had the time to actually partner with clients to bring about positive change in their lives. After all, the reason people take these jobs is because they want to help people. If less time is required to navigate a needlessly complex system, they might have that luxury. Labour unions still have a role to play today, but that role has changed. The programs that address the particular needs of specific neighbourhoods and groups of people are still very necessary. Everyone needs enough money to live a modest but comfortable life, and a basic income can deliver money far more efficiently than its alternatives. However, money alone will not solve all the ills of the world. There will always be a need for people to deliver specific programs for particular groups of people with special needs.

Overcoming Taxpayer Resistance

It is challenging for some people to accept that basic income, important and beneficial as it is, will not pay for itself. Basic income is a program of income redistribution. Even if a basic income costs no more than $23 billion a year, some set of taxpayers will have to send more money to the government than they do now to pay for it. Imagining that we can somehow wrestle enough money out of the notorious "1 per cent" is fanciful; even though the extremely wealthy have obscene amounts of money, there are simply not enough of them to pay all the costs of a basic income. We will not be able to find $23 billion a year by eliminating waste or being more efficient. Of course, the wealthiest people in Canada should pay all the taxes they are legally obligated to pay, but it is the people whose incomes fall in the highest 20 per cent of household incomes who will pay higher taxes to finance the program.

These people are not plutocrats; they are small business owners, professionals like doctors, accountants and lawyers, university professors, some media people and employees of foundations and think tanks. They are people who work hard to provide for themselves and their families, who pay their taxes, and who struggle to balance their work obligations with the rest of their lives. These taxpayers are also very vocal and well connected. It is only reasonable that we should expect them to protect their own interests, and that they should ask questions about why additional tax revenue is necessary. However, they — we — are not the victims of globalization and technology that we sometimes imagine ourselves to be. Those of us with incomes in the top 20 per cent have benefited disproportionately from the economic changes in recent decades that have created new opportunities for work and investment. Yet we still worry about our futures and those of our children, who work hard to find permanent, well-paying jobs, buy modest houses and pay for daycare. Paying for a basic income will not be painless.

If we design our measures appropriately, the people who will pay higher taxes will be relatively high-income individuals who can best afford the cost, but they will see themselves as middle class. Many will believe that they, alone, are responsible for their success, forgetting the investments that society made in the schools and universities that gave them the capacity to earn high incomes. We don't often remember that the tax code has been written to allow us to protect some of our income and assets (in the forms of dividends and capital gains, for example) at the expense of others without the capacity to make use of such tax expenditures. We forget that our high incomes are only possible because all taxpayers have invested in the infrastructure that makes the businesses we create feasible and lucrative, and in ensuring that the rule of law protects our property and our communities. It is time to ask ourselves whether we want our tax system to continue to favour the relatively well off — the professional and business classes — or whether we want to shift taxes just a bit to reinstate the progressivity that will allow every person in Canada a better opportunity to reach his or her full capacity. There is, I believe, an appetite in this country to examine our entire tax system. Some of the pressure is coming from the well off, who look to the United States and somehow feel that their taxes ought to be reduced even more to help them stay competitive. Some of the pressure is coming from ordinary middle- and upper-middle-class people who wonder why their neighbours, who happen to be professionals like doctors or lawyers, can somehow arrange to have a salary paid into their corporation and transform their income into capital gains taxed at lower rates. Little of the pressure is coming from low-income people who are trying to stay afloat because they recognize, quite rightly, that over the past two decades, tax reform has disproportionately benefited higher-income people.

Taxpayers are more likely to accept a tax if they believe it is applied fairly, and if the revenue from that tax is invested in something important. Accountability is a fair request. But accountability does not mean policing the expenditure or behaviour of individual families who receive a basic income. There are many examples of self-righteous scrutiny being passed off as "accountability." For example, in 2014, under Governor Paul LePage, the state of Maine decided to investigate families who received cash benefits through a federal program called Temporary Assistance for Needy Families (TANF). These benefits are loaded onto debit cards that leave a digital record of when and where cash is withdrawn. The administration identified 3,650 transactions in which TANF recipients used ATMs in smoke shops, liquor stores and out-of-state locations. Then they released the data to the public, suggesting that TANF recipients were defrauding taxpayers by buying liquor, cigarettes and lottery tickets. Policymakers and the professional middle class then pushed the legislature to introduce a bill that would require all TANF families to keep all cash receipts for twelve months for audit purposes, and urged the governor to use the list to prosecute recipients for fraud. The "suspicious" transactions constituted only 0.3 per cent of the 1.1 million transactions during the period, and the record shows only where the money was withdrawn, and not what was purchased with the funds. Nevertheless, the purpose of the exercise was to stigmatize those who use social programs, and to reinforce the story that recipients are criminal, lazy, spendthrift addicts.[2]

When the Ford government in Ontario decided to cancel the Ontario basic income pilot, the minister of social services simultaneously announced that she had asked the Auditor General to investigate "hundreds of millions of dollars" in fraud in social assistance payments. She offered no evidence to support the allegation. This is not what I mean by accountability.

Accountability means that a government should commit to transparent reporting of the costs of a program and progress made toward clearly stated social goals. This might seem obvious, but it is not now an easy task to find the costs associated with income support. The Parliamentary Budget Office noted that the federal government spent $122 billion for tax expenditures in 2017 — $122 billion in tax credits that are not subject to program evaluations. There is no program of regular or ongoing examination to determine whether these tax expenditures meet their goals, or whether they give us good value for their cost. By contrast, federal program expenditures undergo regular evaluations. Provincial expenditures on income assistance are not knowable with certainty, even though many provinces have committed to "transparent government," because payments are aggregated with other expenditures, and the administrative costs are not identified.

Since neither provincial nor federal governments report their expenditures in clear and useful ways, no one should be surprised that many taxpayers assume their tax payments disappear into great dark holes. Any taxpayer should be able to find out what programs cost, how the costs change over time, how many people benefit and whether beneficiaries are old or young, male or female, in families or living alone. We should know whether the programs meet the needs of families that receive support, and what proportion of families becomes more independent over time.

Taxes used to support government programs can be levied in many ways, and it is reasonable to expect taxes to be efficient and well administered. Raising taxes to support basic income does not necessarily mean raising marginal income tax rates or even corporate taxes. There are many different kinds of taxes, but one place to begin is with the list of tax expenditures — $122 billion a year, remember, at the federal level alone — compiled by the Parliamentary Budget Office. Some of these expenditures are necessary and useful; others have lost whatever purpose they may once have had.

We do not need to wait for a review of the entire tax system to implement a basic income. There are several options available. However, any review of the tax system should have, as one goal, the identification of an income stream to support a fair and equitable basic income.

One Way Forward

The benefits of a basic income are undeniable, as are the fiscal challenges facing all Canadian provinces. The Parliamentary Budget Office has effectively demolished the claim that Canada cannot afford a basic income of the type that Ontario began to pilot. The argument that a basic income will discourage people from working has been challenged by current and past basic income experiments that showed that any reduction in work effort was generally associated with investments in education that will pay off over the long run. Ongoing experiments around the world will generate additional evidence that a basic income will both improve lives and reduce the costs of other social programs without discouraging work. They will also give us a good sense of what other supports are necessary for some people, and how basic income fits into the larger social-services landscape.

Progress toward a national basic income in Canada, however, can only come about with the leadership of the federal government. It should open negotiations with the provinces and First Nations with the goal of designing and implementing a national basic income that meets Canadian needs. Such a program is both feasible and necessary.

The federal government, however, need not wait for the outcome of these negotiations to address the issue. It can introduce a small basic income for adults — smaller than the Ontario guarantee and consistent with whatever is prudent in the current economic climate — but with very clear goals to raise the real value of the guarantee to the target level over a reasonable period of time. Both the target and the timeline should be identified to Canadians, who can hold the government to account at election time. Federal payments would not reduce eligibility for provincial income assistance and could be delivered in a very cost-effective way through the income tax system. Ongoing efforts to ensure all adults complete income tax forms should be strengthened. At the same time, the federal government should commit to identifying the ongoing costs of the program and its outcomes. Outcome measures can be identified by an oversight committee established by the federal government. Plain-language reports should be prepared annually for all taxpayers.

As negotiations between governments continue, and people begin to benefit from the basic income, the provinces will begin to recognize the opportunities available to them. If pressure on the health care system is reduced because of basic income, the provinces will be the major beneficiaries. A greater proportion of provincial support can be reallocated to job training and life skills courses, enhanced health benefits, daycare and education.

At the same time, the federal government will be under less pressure to increase the Canada Health Transfer and the Canada Social Transfer to the provinces since the benefits of a basic income can be expected to relieve pressure on provincial social programs. Over time, the lumbering and old-fashioned Canadian income tax system might even begin to be modernized, so that the federal government would have a greater capacity to adjust the basic income more regularly to meet the changing needs of families. If that happened, provincial income assistance could be reduced to a much smaller program, focused on special cases and emergencies, with the bulk of provincial funding going to support real programs focused on local needs.

The federal government would do what a federal government does best — collect taxes and transfer money. Provincial, local and First Nations governments, who are arguably closer to the people and more aware of local circumstances and needs, could focus on delivering specific programs and meeting unique needs.

Basic income is feasible. It is not a theoretical construct with no possibility of real-world application. We can afford it, and we need not wait for all the various parts of an unwieldy political system to initiate it. Basic income requires the leadership of the federal government.

There Is No Perfect Time: Let's Begin Now

The temptation to wait before we embark on a bold, new social program until "the time is right" is deeply ingrained. Even if basic income is a good idea, we are cautioned, we can't introduce it now because the economy is unstable and everybody already feels like they pay too much in taxes. We must wait until we can afford it. Except . . . we can never afford it. There is always another new reason to delay. There is always another new expenditure that must take precedence. After all, we've lived with poverty and economic insecurity for millennia — what's another couple of years or decades?

We can rest a case for basic income on social justice or compassion. We can argue that accelerating economic change is increasing the number of people who would benefit from a basic income. We might point to the social divisions in American society as a cautionary tale, and suggest that basic income is one way to quell social unrest. We can even make an economic case: we already pay so much to deliver social programs to treat the effects of poverty and economic insecurity. Basic income simply suggests that we invest some of that expenditure upstream so that the worst effects of economic insecurity are eliminated before they happen. But all these arguments inevitably face the claim that we cannot undertake even the modest expenditure associated with a basic income because the United States might cut taxes and we have no choice but to follow, or because trade agreements might founder and have negative consequences for the Canadian economy, or simply because it is impossible to raise taxes.

A $23 billion annual expenditure for basic income is not unaffordable in a wealthy country like Canada. It does not require massive tax increases, dramatic deficits or class warfare. We absorbed the Canada Child Benefit with no ill effects; in fact, the initial economic consequences seem largely positive. We consider pharmacare or national daycare programs of the same magnitude. It's time to consider basic income.

Chapter 11
A Basic Income for All of Us

Basic income is about more than welfare reform. Basic income benefits all Canadians.

Certainly, people who now depend on provincial income assistance and disability support will gain from a predictable income sufficient to allow them to live a modest but comfortable life. They will have the freedom to make decisions on behalf of their families without bureaucratic intervention, and the opportunity to plan better lives for themselves and their children. A basic income addresses deprivation at its source while the current system waits to address the consequences of poverty by spending more on our health care system, special education, child services and the justice system.

However, the greatest beneficiaries of basic income are those of us who do not currently receive provincial income assistance. Basic income is an insurance policy that protects us against life events. Any one of us can get sick or develop a disability at any point in our lives. Any one of us can have a child with disabilities who alters all our well-laid plans. Any one of us may be called upon to provide extra care for a parent or spouse who becomes ill. People used to living an ordinary middle-class life find out quickly enough how much changes when they become dependent on provincial support at current rates. Even those of us who have been lucky enough to have worked at a good job and responsible enough to save money for the future may find ourselves retired a decade before we planned to leave the workforce, or downsized mid-career in an industry we expected to give us lifelong employment. Those who had the foresight to save their money while they were working are doubly disadvantaged; their assets will exceed those permitted by provincial income assistance, and they will be required to spend their savings before they qualify for provincial support. A lifetime of working to save for a comfortable retirement can disappear in a flash.

The changing economy means that more and more of us, especially younger adults, are working at jobs organized in very different ways than they used to be. We may face decades of contract work or multiple part-time jobs. Job insecurity might leave contingent workers for long or short periods of time with no income and little money saved. Women, especially, are still subject to the hard clock of biology. Extended maternity and parental leaves are wonderful for people who manage to work enough hours to qualify for support, but many do not qualify because they have lived through extended periods of insecure and part-time work. How do you build a family while relying on precarious work to support yourself?

Life happens.

Everyone benefits from basic income whether they receive support from the program or not, in exactly the same way that all Canadians benefit from universal health insurance even if they do not now need hospital care, and in exactly the same way we benefit from fire insurance even if our house doesn't burn down. Basic income is an insurance policy against unpredictable life events.

The cost estimates provided by the Parliamentary Budget Office demonstrate that we can afford to provide Canadians with this insurance. Just as it now seems inconceivable that we would ever allow ordinary people in Canada to be bankrupted by the need for hospital care, one day we will wonder why ordinary working people were required to shoulder all the uncertainties associated with life in a changing economy alone.

There are other benefits of a basic income that we also need to acknowledge. Poverty — whether it's the chronic, grinding and absolute poverty of some isolated First Nations communities, the relative poverty faced by the children of a single mother in urban Canada, or the many challenges faced by middle-aged adults living alone — is tremendously expensive. It is a false economy to deprive people of the resources they need to live a decent life because we as taxpayers have no choice but to pay for the consequences in the form of health care for their chronic conditions that will get worse with poor diets and poor housing. We have no choice but to pay for the costs of foster care when children are removed from homes because their parents do not have the resources to care appropriately for their families. We will pay for special education when families do not have enough money to provide stable and adequate housing for their children, and send them to school well-fed. The costs of poverty are avoidable. While the primary beneficiaries of a basic income may be the families who receive support, taxpayers will benefit as well.

We can continue to allocate our money to the agencies that mop up the effects of years of inadequate diets, inadequate housing, demeaning work and poor education in the form of greater health care expenditure, more money for child welfare services, breakfast programs in schools and more food banks. We can fund more mental health centres and addiction agencies charged with treating the consequences of poverty and marginalization. We can reap the social consequences in terms of rising property crime rates and greater alienation. We can watch as populist political candidates prey on the disaffection of our neighbours. Or we can look at our social programs in this country and acknowledge that we are less generous than most other high-income countries, and that we have the capacity to offer a basic income to Canadians if we want to.

Despite its benefits and demonstrated feasibility, basic income remains a controversial proposal in Canada. Many of us, especially those of us who are middle-class professionals, want to believe that we are not vulnerable — that people who access social programs are very different from the rest of us. Recognizing our own vulnerability and that of our children is frightening. The idea of a basic income raises for us a series of profound questions that we rarely confront openly — questions about how we relate to one another in society. However, most people who need the support of a basic income are ordinary people who have faced some unexpected setbacks. The only difference between those who would receive support under a basic income and the rest of us is that they have less money.

When I began working my way through the 1,800 cardboard boxes related to Mincome at Library and Archives Canada, very few people in this country were talking about basic income. Between the time I opened the first box and the time I published my first analysis of the health effects of Mincome in 2011, stock markets tumbled in the wake of the 2008 financial meltdown. The shock spread through the economy as firms went bankrupt, and workers found themselves without jobs and, in many cases, with compromised pensions. A lifetime of loyalty to an employer seemed to count for little. And, worst of all, the social programs that were supposed to provide a safety net — Employment Insurance, the Canada Pension Plan and provincial income assistance as a last resort — weren't available to many of the people who found themselves needing help, sometimes for the first time in their lives.

In the context of that economic upheaval, the story of a little prairie town called Dauphin captured the imaginations of people around the world. I've been fortunate enough to talk to people in places as different as Finland, Portugal, Korea and Norway. I've told stories about the people who participated in Mincome to audiences in Paris and Geneva. I've travelled across Canada and the United States, speaking in church basements and lecture theatres, town halls and hotel ballrooms. Everyone is captivated by the idea of a very ordinary little town that experimented with basic income and eager to hear of its effects on the lives of the strong, hardworking and very ordinary people who lived there. Most of these people were not on welfare when Mincome came along. They were farmers and labourers, hairdressers and shopkeepers. When Mincome was introduced, they were able to offer their children more opportunities and to plan for their futures with greater certainty. But they were still farmers and labourers, hairdressers and shopkeepers. They didn't quit their jobs, and their lives didn't change dramatically. Things just got a bit easier for ordinary people who worked really hard to provide for themselves and their families.

When universal health insurance was introduced in Canada, its greatest support came from middle-aged women — people who had lived long enough to know that life doesn't always unfold according to plan. I think it is telling that the strongest and most vocal support for basic income also comes from middle-aged women, whether they live in Tampere or Seoul, Barcelona or Dauphin.

We can afford a basic income. The logistics of implementation are not insurmountable. It is merely a question of will. Do we want to offer one another the economic security a basic income can provide?

Appendix:
Notes on the cost of a basic income

Cost Estimates

The cost of a simple basic income in Canada depends on three variables: the size of the basic income guarantee for those with no other income; the rate at which basic income will be reduced as private income increases; and the behavioural responses of individuals as they react to taxes. If people work fewer hours as a basic income is introduced, the costs of the program will increase because more people will receive more of the basic income. If the basic income guarantee is increased, the cost will increase. If the tax-back rate — the speed with which the basic income declines as private income increases — increases, the cost will decline. One way of estimating these costs is to use a microsimulation model developed by Statistics Canada called the Social Policy Simulation Database and Model (SPSD/M). This is the method adopted by the Parliamentary Budget Office. SPSD/M is an accounting model used by various levels of government to make budget projections. It does not include behavioural responses, so results will have to be adjusted to incorporate the extent to which people can be expected to work less when basic income is introduced. Something that becomes very clear is that the precise specification of how the basic income will operate is very important.

David Macdonald has estimated the upfront costs of a variety of basic income formulations extended to the entire country. He begins by identifying some thirty-three existing low-income support programs; most are provincial, but he includes OAS/GIS, the federal Canada Child Benefit and the GST credit. These programs will cost federal and provincial governments a projected $82.9 billion in 2016, rising to $108.7 billion if we include social assistance and Employment Insurance. These amounts do not include administrative costs. Macdonald chooses to replace all these programs with a variety of basic income formulations. For our purpose, we will focus on his negative income tax or targeted basic income formulation. The cost estimation that comes closest to the basic income that was piloted in Ontario but extended to the entire country is Macdonald's Scenario 6: social assistance is added to the list of existing programs and tax credits that would be cancelled to make room for a basic income worth $17,080 for those who need it most.[1] There is no net cost to the government, although provincial costs are shifted to the federal government in this scheme. Macdonald's simulation produces reductions in the overall poverty rates for children under eighteen and especially adults, but the poverty rate among seniors increases because the simulation replaces Old Age Security and the Guaranteed Income Supplement with a basic income that provides less. The Ontario formulation does not apply to seniors who are assumed to have continued access to OAS/GIS while Macdonald's scheme transfers income from seniors to younger people. Net losers under Macdonald's scheme are mostly high-income families that currently benefit from the Canada Child Benefit and the Old Age Security pension, but also include some low-income people (especially women) over sixty-five who currently benefit from the relatively generous support offered to seniors. Labour supply responses were not included, and, to the extent that people work less under a basic income, the effective cost will increase.

Taking seniors out of the scheme reduces the number of people who receive a basic income but also reduces the money that would otherwise be redistributed by the cost of OAS/GIS programs. Setting the basic income guarantee to the Ontario levels (no adjustment for children and reduced entitlements for couples), extending it to the entire country and retaining the Canada Child Benefit and OAS/GIS will reduce its net costs, although the precise amount will depend on the assumptions one makes about tax-back rates and the treatment of income from existing programs. As in the case above, however, the savings revert to provincial governments in the form of reduced income assistance, but the costs are imposed on the federal government. Once again, costs would increase if labour supply declined in response to a basic income.

Robin Boadway, Katherine Cuff and Kourtney Koebel propose a revenue-neutral basic income that would significantly improve the relative position of those in the bottom of the net income distribution and reduce poverty. Their nationwide proposal would replace existing non-refundable and refundable tax credits. Social insurance programs such as Employment Insurance, Workers' Compensation and Canada and Quebec Pension Plans would remain. Notably, they also allow for a reduction in the number of people working when a basic income is introduced. Once again, single seniors gain least by the change since they currently benefit most from existing transfers. Boadway and his colleagues note that tax-back rates need not be onerous to make the system cost neutral.[2]

Different basic income schemes have been proposed by Derek Hum and Wayne Simpson, Margot Young and James P. Mulvale, Harvey Simpson and Wayne Stevens and Charles Lammam and Hugh MacIntyre.[3] These proposals differ in terms of income guarantee levels, tax-back rates and the degree to which existing programs will be eliminated. For example, Lammam and MacIntyre replaced all programs addressed to income support, including Employment Insurance, Canada and Quebec Pension Plans and social assistance in the interest of saving administrative costs; their scheme is similar to the proposal offered by Milton Friedman.

Can We Offer a Universal Basic Income and Get It All Back Through Taxes?

Outside Canada, the most common formulation of a basic income is a universal basic income, or UBI, that offers everyone, rich or poor, the same monthly payment. This payment, unlike the targeted formulation we have discussed in Canada, is taxable. This has led some of the more strident international advocates to argue that there is no financial difference between a targeted scheme and a UBI because high-income earners "pay it all back in taxes." These advocates go on to argue that low-income earners will be net recipients because they pay less in total taxes than they receive through a basic income while high-income earners become net payers because they pay more in total taxes than they receive in basic income. This argument is misleading.

In Canada, top income earners face a combined provincial and federal income tax rate of approximately 50 per cent — a little more in some provinces, and a bit less in others. If one of these top income earners receives a basic income of twenty thousand dollars a year, she will pay half of it to the Canada Revenue Agency in the form of income tax. She keeps ten thousand dollars of the basic income. This is true no matter how high her income is: her top marginal rate never reaches 100 per cent, and therefore, she will never pay it all back in taxes. If she spends the money, she will pay a bit more additional tax in the form of provincial and federal sales taxes. However, she will never pay it all back.

There are only two ways to "get it all back in taxes" and make the net costs of the two approaches identical. The first is the way we tax Old Age Security to ensure that top earners do not benefit from the program. We levy a special recovery tax on Old Age Security income only, and as of 2018, it reaches 100 per cent when income from other sources reaches $123,019. There is no more furious Canadian than someone over sixty-five who has received Old Age Security only to be told that he must pay it all back at income tax time in April. To avoid this, we calculate eligibility upfront and do not send payments to people likely to exceed the maximum. This effectively turns our "universal" Old Age Security into a targeted benefit. Using this approach, a UBI and a targeted basic income would be identical because we would have turned the UBI into a targeted program. This is not what UBI advocates had in mind.

The only other way to ensure that a UBI is returned in tax revenue by high-income earners is to raise taxes significantly above current rates on those high-income earners. If we retain the current marginal tax rate system, this can only happen by eliminating tax expenditures — tax deductions and non-refundable tax credits — from which high-income earners currently benefit. This can certainly be done, but it is more than a little disingenuous to claim that the tax system will recover the UBI sent to high-income earners. It happens only because we are raising taxes rather significantly.

We can certainly make the net costs of a universal basic income and a targeted basic income look the same. The difference is that with a universal basic income, a much greater proportion of economic activity is funneled through the government. Government expenditure increases by the (much larger) gross cost of a universal basic income, and tax revenue must increase by the same amount to pay for it. In the end, Canadians (on average) have the same amount of money in their pockets whichever approach we take, but I doubt that we are indifferent to the total size of government expenditure and taxation. The Ontario targeted basic income program rolled out nationally would cost $23 billion annually. A universal basic income that would provide approximately the same level of support would require current federal government expenditure to almost double, with tax revenue almost doubling to pay for it. High-income earners in particular would resist the latter.

Acknowledgements

I am very grateful for the many, many people who helped me with this project. I'd like to thank Stephenson Strobel who acted as a research assistant for several years. The "two Davids" at Library and Archives Canada put up with my requests for access, and the many requests of journalists and documentary filmmakers who wanted to "film the boxes." Eric Richardson was a willing subject for many journalists, and an entrée into Dauphin society. Richard Lobdell, Barbara Boraks and Sheila Regehr read and criticized this manuscript, and for that I am very thankful. I'd also like to thank Hugh Segal who hosted me at Massey College during the 2015–16 academic year as a Kierans-Janigan Visiting Scholar. CIHR (MOP-110984) and SSHRC (435-2015-1075) supported some of the research on which this book is based. I am also grateful to James Lorimer, Jim Turk, Carrie Gleason, Scott Fraser, Sara D'Agostino and William Brown at Lorimer.

Further Reading

Chapter 1

Many books have been published on the idea of basic income and approach the topic from a variety of perspectives. Of the following, some are very accessible while others provide a more complex, scholarly discussion of basic income.

Bregman, Rutger. *Utopia for Realists: The Case for a Universal Basic Income, Open Borders, and a 15-Hour Work Week.* Amsterdam: The Correspondent, 2016.
> This book, by a Dutch historian, is great fun to read. It is provocative, as its subtitle suggests, and very well written. Bregman focuses on a universal basic income (as opposed to a targeted benefit) and challenges us to imagine a future much different from the past.

Hughes, Chris. *Fair Shot: Rethinking Inequality and How We Earn.* London: Bloomsbury, 2018.
> Chris Hughes (a Facebook co-founder) argues, in a well-written and entertaining book, that one-percenters like him should pay for a guaranteed income for everyone. He advocates a targeted benefit similar to the one adopted by Ontario for its pilot, which he provides support for in the book.

Lewchuk, Wayne, and Marlea Clarke. *Working Without Commitments: The Health Effects of Precarious Employment.* Montreal: McGill-Queen's University Press, 2011.
Lewchuk, Wayne, Michelynn LaFlèche, Diane Dyson, et al. 2013. *It's More than Poverty: Employment Precarity and Employment Well-Being.* Poverty and Employment Precarity in Southern Ontario (PEPSO).
> Wayne Lewchuk is the Canadian expert on precarious employment. The book by Lewchuk and Clarke emphasizes the effects of precarity on health and well-being.

Standing, Guy. *Basic Income and How We Can Make It Happen.* Pelican Books, 2017.
Standing, Guy. *The Precariat: The New Dangerous Class.* London: Bloomsbury, 2011.
> Guy Standing is the international expert on the rise of the precariat — the insecurely employed underclass in today's economy — and a well-known advocate for basic income, which he, too, defines as a universal basic income given equally to everyone, rich or poor. The first book is intended as an entry-level account of the debate and is broadly accessible and the second focuses more closely on the economic effects of precarious labour.

Stern, Andy. *Raising the Floor: How a Universal Basic Income Can Renew Our Economy and Rebuild the American Dream.* New York: PublicAffairs, 2016.
> This book, by a well-known labour leader, focuses on changes in the labour market, especially in the United States, and suggests that a universal basic income — a flat payment to everyone, rich or poor — is the appropriate way to renew the economy and rebuild the American dream.

Van Parijs, Philippe, and Yannick Vanderborght. *Basic Income: A Radical Proposal for a Free Society and a Sane Economy.* Cambridge, MA: Harvard University Press, 2017.
> This is a much more scholarly account of the debate that approaches the topic from the perspective of freedom. This book also treats universal basic income as the ideal.

Chapter 2

Baird, Sarah, Craig McIntosh, and Berk Özler. "Cash or Condition? Evidence from a Cash Transfer Experiment." *Quarterly Journal of Economics* 126, no. 4 (2011):1709–53.
A cash transfer program was established in Malawi, with some dramatic health results. This experiment compared a cash transfer that families received if they sent their adolescent daughters to school to a cash transfer that families received unconditionally. As might be expected, the conditional cash transfer was more successful at encouraging families to send their daughters to school, but an unintended outcome occurred in the unconditional arm that did not occur in the conditional arm: the incidence of HIV declined, and this was attributed to the fact that transactional sex work among girls in the poorest families declined when families received support. A discussion of the results and their relevance to the BI debate in Canada is available here:

Forget, Evelyn L., Alexander D. Peden, and Stephenson B. Strobel. "Cash Transfers, Basic Income and Community Building." *Social Inclusion* 1, no. 2 (2013): 84–91. http://www.cogitatiopress.com/ojs/index.php/socialinclusion/article/view/113.
Forget, Evelyn L. "New Questions, New data, Old interventions: The Health Effects of a Guaranteed Annual Income." *Journal of Preventive Medicine* 57, no. 6 (2013): 925–28. doi: 10.1016/j.ypmed.2013.05.029.
Forget, Evelyn L. "The Town with No Poverty: The Health Effects of a Canadian Guaranteed Annual Income Field Experiment." *Canadian Public Policy* 37, no. 3 (2011): 283–305.
The Dauphin site of Mincome is responsible for broadening the debate over basic income in high-income countries to a consideration of health and well-being.

Owusu-Addo, Ebenezer, Andre M.N. Renzaho, and Ben J. Smith. "The Impact of Cash Transfers on Social Determinants of Health and Health Inequalities in Sub-Saharan Africa: A Systematic Review." *Health Policy and Planning* 5, no. 114 (2018). https://doi.org/10.1093/heapol/czy020.
We should be careful about generalizing from the results of basic income (or cash transfer) programs in low- and middle-income countries, but the above is an excellent review of the health outcomes of a variety of such experiments in sub-Saharan Africa.

Chapter 3

Martin, Danielle. *Better Now? Six Big Ideas to Improve Health Care for All Canadians.* Toronto: Penguin Canada, 2016.
The relationship between poverty and poor health is pervasive. Almost any area of health is worsened by poverty. An interesting and accessible account is available in this book by Danielle Martin, who recounts her experiences in family medicine.

Raphael, David. *Social Determinants of Health: Canadian Perspectives, 2nd edition.* Toronto: Canadian Scholars' Press, 2009.
A good discussion of the social determinants of health in a Canadian context is available here.

Wilkinson, Richard G., and Kate Pickett. *The Spirit Level: Why Equality Is Better for Everyone.* London: Penguin, 2010.
An accessible discussion of the role played by inequality on health outcomes is available in this very popular book.

The effects of chronic stress on long-term heath are also very well-documented in the medical literature:

Baum, Andrew, J.P. Garofalo, and Ann Marie Yali. "Socioeconomic Status and Chronic Stress: Does Stress Account for SES Effects on Health?" *Annals of the New York Academy of Sciences* 896 (1999): 131–44.

Cohen, Sheldon, Denise Janicki-Deverts, William J. Doyle, Gregory E. Miller, Ellen Frank, Bruce S. Rabin, and Ronald B. Turner. "Chronic Stress, Glucocorticoid Receptor Resistance, Inflammation, and Disease Risk." *Proceedings of the National Academy of Sciences* 109, no. 16 (2012): 5995–99.

Dickerson, Sally S., and Margaret E. Kemeny. "Acute Stressors and Cortisol Responses: A Theoretical Integration and Synthesis of Laboratory Research." *Psychological Bulletin* 130 (2004): 355–91

Epel, Elissa S., Elizabeth H. Blackburn, Jue Lin, Firdaus S. Dhabhar, Nancy E. Adler, Jason D. Morrow, and Richard M. Cawthon. "Accelerated Telomere Shortening in Response to Life Stress." *Proceedings of the National Academy of Sciences of the United States of America* 101, no. 49 (2004): 17312–15.

Kopp, Mária S., and János Réthelyi. "Where Psychology Meets Physiology: Chronic Stress and Premature Mortality — The Central-Eastern European Health Paradox." *Brain Research Bulletin* 62, no. 5 (2004): 351–67.

Layte, Richard, and Christopher Whelan. 2013. GINI DP 78: "Who Feels Inferior? A Test of the Status Anxiety Hypothesis of Social Inequalities in Health." GINI Discussion Paper 78, AIAS, Amsterdam Institute for Advanced Labour Studies, Amsterdam, Netherlands, 2013.

Loughnan, Steve, Peter Kuppens, Jüri Allik, Katalin Balazs, Soledad de Lemus, Kitty Dumont, et al. "Economic Inequality Is Linked to Biased Self-Perception." *Psychological Science* 22 (2011): 1254–58.

Marin, Marie-France, Catherine Lord, Julie Andrews, Robert-Paul Juster, Shireen Sindi, Geneviève Arsenault-Lapierre, Alexandra J. Fiocco, and Sonia J. Lupien. "Chronic Stress, Cognitive Functioning and Mental Health." *Neurobiology of Learning and Memory* 96, no. 4 (2011): 583–95.

Mitchell, Colter, John Hobcraft, Sarah S. McLanahan, Susan Rutherford Siegel, Arthur Berg, Jeanne Brooks-Gunn, Irwin Garfinkel, and Daniel Notterman. "Social Disadvantage, Genetic Sensitivity, and Children's Telomere Length." *Proceedings of the National Academy of Sciences* 111, no. 16 (2014): 5944–49.

Steptoe, Andrew, and Pamela J. Feldman. "Neighborhood Problems as Sources of Chronic Stress: Development of a Measure of Neighborhood Problems, and Associations with Socioeconomic Status and Health. *Annals of Behavioral Medicine* 23, no. 3 (2001): 177–85.

Chapter 4

Brynjolfsson, Erik, and Andrew McAfee. *The Second Machine Age: Work Progress and Prosperity in a Time of Brilliant Technologies.* New York: WW Norton, 2014.

Ford, Martin. *Rise of the Robots: Technology and the Threat of a Jobless Future.* New York: Basic Books, 2016.
Excellent discussions of a future without work can be found in both of the above titles.

David Graeber. *Bullshit Jobs: A Theory.* New York: Simon & Schuster, 2018.
This is an entertaining read on the nature of jobs. Graeber effectively questions the

identification of "work" with jobs that are accessed through the market for pay. He puts care work and artistic endeavour at the centre of human existence.

Lamb, Creig. 2016. *The Talented Mr. Robot: The Impact of Automation on Canada's Workforce.* Toronto: Brookfield Institute for Innovation + Entrepreneurship, 2016. http://brookfieldinstitute.ca/wp-content/uploads/2016/07/TheTalentedMrRobotReport.pdf.
The challenges to the way we work brought about by technological change are pervasive in the popular literature. Lamb's text is an enjoyable read on this subject.

By contrast, if you are interested in the standard line that we are in the midst of a labour shortage, you'll find a plethora of articles in the business press. Newspaper articles and commentaries on Canada's imagined labour shortage are easy to find. The Canadian Federation of Independent Business sparked this article in *Huffington Post*:
Tencer, Daniel. "Canada's Labour Shortage Intensifies, with Nearly 400,000 Vacant Jobs." *Huffington Post*, March 13, 2018. https://www.huffingtonpost.ca/2018/03/13/labour-shortage-canada-job-vacancies_a_23384818/.

Nearly simultaneously, a horde of articles declaring that "robots will take our jobs" appeared, for example:
Elliott, Larry. "Robots Will Take Our Jobs. We'd Better Plan Now Before It's Too Late." *The Guardian*, February 1, 2018. https://www.theguardian.com/commentisfree/2018/feb/01/robots-take-our-jobs-amazon-go-seattle.

Chapter 5

Ariely, D. *Predictably Irrational. The Hidden Forces That Shape Our Decisions.* New York: HarperCollins, 2008.
Dan Ariely can be found on TED Talks. This book is of particular relevance.

Folbre, Nancy. *The Invisible Heart: Economics and Family Values.* New York: New Press, 2001.
Nancy Folbre has written a wonderful work on caring labour in the United States.

Loney, Shaun, with Will Braun. *An Army of Problem Solvers: Reconciliation and the Solutions Economy.* Altona, MB: Friesens, 2016.

Skidelsky, Robert, and Edward Skidelsky. *How Much is Enough? Money and the Good Life.* London: Penguin, 2012.
Others see basic income as a means of constraining our over-consuming lifestyles. Robert and Edward Skidelsky pick up the themes addressed by John Maynard Keynes (*Economic Opportunities for our Grandchildren*) and John Stuart Mill. All examine the philosophical underpinnings of economics and ask what kind of a society we want to create.

Srnicek, Nick, and Alex Williams. 2015. *Inventing the Future: Postcapitalism and a World Without Work.* New York: Verso, 2015.
If you want to explore post-work imaginaries and the call for a new socialist imagination, try this one.

Chapter 6

A special issue of *Basic Income Studies* published in December 2008 (Volume 3, Issue 3), entitled "Should Feminists Endorse Basic Income?" published varying perspectives.

Readers might also enjoy reading:

McKay, Ailsa. "Rethinking Work and Income Maintenance Policy: Promoting Gender Equality Through a Citizens' Basic Income." *Feminist Economics* 7, no. 1 (2001): pp.97–118.

McKay, Ailsa. "Why a Citizens' Basic Income? A Question of Gender Equality or Gender Bias." *Work, Employment and Society* 21, no. 2 (2007): 337–48.

Regehr, Sheila. 2014. "Basic Income and Gender Equality: Reflections on the Potential for Good Policy in Canada." http://www.basicincome.org/bien/pdf/montreal2014/BIEN2014_Regehr. pdf.

Reynolds, Tracey. "Black Women, Gender Equality and Universal Basic Income." *Compass* (blog), January 27, 2017. https://www.compassonline.org.uk/black-women-gender-equality-and-universal-basic-income/.

Chapter 7

Nordström Skans, Oskar. "Scarring Effects of the First Labor Market Experience." IZA Discussion Paper, No. 5565, IZA — Institute of Labour Economics, Bonn, Germany, 2011.

The literature on labour scarring is fairly technical and is mostly buried in economics journals, but this paper is particularly useful for understanding its effects.

Chapter 8

Bregman, Rutger. *Utopia for Realists: The Case for a Universal Basic Income, Open Borders, and a 15-Hour Work Week.* Amsterdam: The Correspondent, 2016.

This chapter has taken a very clear position that basic income is a simply a policy of redistribution, not different in kind from many other similar policies that we have already chosen to implement. This is a much more modest position than that taken by Rutger Bregman, who speculates in this book about a very different kind of world in which basic income plays a part.

Chapter 9

Boadway, Robin W., Katherine Cuff, and Kourtney Koebel. *Designing a basic income guarantee for Canada.* Working Paper No. 1371, Economics Department, Queen's University, Kingston, Ontario, 2016.

"Costing a National Guaranteed Basic Income Using the Ontario Basic Income Model." Ottawa: Office of the Parliamentary Budget Officer, April 17, 2018.

"Federal Support for Low Income Families and Children." Ottawa: Office of the Parliamentary Budget Officer, 2017.

Lammam, Charles, and Hugh MacIntyre H. *The Practical Challenges of Creating a Guaranteed Annual Income.* Vancouver: Fraser Institute, 2015.

Macdonald, David. "A Policymaker's Guide to Basic Income." Ottawa: Canadian Centre for Policy Alternatives, 2016. See Appendix for further discussion.

Stevens, Harvey, and Wayne Simpson. "Toward a National Universal Guaranteed Basic Income." *Canadian Public Policy* (2017): 120–39.

Endnotes

Chapter 1

1. Department of Finance Canada, "Backgrounder: Strengthening the Canada Child Benefit," last modified October 24, 2017, https://www.fin.gc.ca/n17/data/17-103_1-eng.asp.
2. However, on October 20, 2017, the Canadian Association of Social Workers proposed that each Canadian receive $20,000, independent of work status. Colleen Kennelly, *Universal Basic Income Guarantee: The Next "BIG" Thing in Canadian Social Policy*, Canadian Association of Social Workers (CASW), October, 2017, https://casw-acts.ca/sites/casw-acts.ca/files/attachements/universal_basic_income_guarantee_the_next_big_thing_in_canadian_social_policy_0.pdf.
3. The idea behind this alternative is that taxes can be increased so that high-income individuals will pay more in taxes than they receive while the poorest receive more than they pay. While mathematically equivalent, this version requires much higher taxes and government expenditures to pay its upfront costs than the targeted version receiving most attention in Canada.
4. John Cunliffe and Guido Erreygers, 2003, "'Basic Income? Basic Capital!' Origins and Issues of a Debate," *Journal of Political Philosophy* 11, no. 1 (2003): 89–110.
    Philippe Van Parijs and Yannick Vanderborght, *Basic Income. A Radical Proposal for a Free Society and a Sane Economy*. Cambridge, MA: Harvard University Press; 2017. See chapters 3 and 4.
5. This limit varies by province and changes over time.
6. This data represents John Stapleton's collation of Ontario Social Assistance administrative data with his data on working poverty. It is reproduced with his permission. There is no simple way to determine how much the provinces spend on income assistance; the data is presented at various levels of aggregation and in quite opaque form. Before its demise, The National Council on Welfare used to track provincial welfare expenditures, but there is no systematic collection currently in place beyond that conducted by John Stapleton.
7. Statistics Canada, Table 282-0080 Labour force survey estimates (LFS), employees by job permanency, North American Industry Classification System (NAICS), sex and age group, annual (persons x 1,000).
8. Stephen Harrington, Jeff Moir, and J. Scott Allinson, *The Intelligence Revolution. Future-Proofing Canada's Workforce*, Deloitte, 2017, https://www2.deloitte.com/content/dam/Deloitte/ca/Documents/human-capital/ca-en-hc-IntelligenceRev-POV-Oct25-AODA.pdf.

Chapter 2

1. For a summary of Mincome in the context of the negative income tax experiments, see: Evelyn L. Forget, "The Town with No Poverty: The Health Effects of a Canadian Guaranteed Annual Income Field Experiment," *Canadian Public Policy* 37, no. 3 (2011): 283–305.
2. See: Canada. 1971a. *Poverty in Canada: Report of the Special Senate Committee on Poverty (Croll Report)*. Ottawa: Information Canada.
    Canada. 1971b. *Welfare Recipients Speak for Themselves (Federal-Provincial Study Group on Alienation)*. Ottawa: Health and Welfare Canada.
    Canada. 1970. *Income Security for Canadians*. Ottawa: Health and Welfare Canada.

3.   Calnitsky, D., 2016. "More Normal than Welfare": The Mincome Experiment, Stigma, and Community Experience. *Canadian Review of Sociology/Revue canadienne de sociologie*, 53(1), pp.26–71.
4.   Derek Hum and Wayne Simpson, *Income Maintenance, Work Effort, and the Canadian Mincome Experiment*, study prepared for the Economic Council of Canada (Ottawa: Canada Communication Group, 1991).
5.   This is what happens for family doctors who are paid a fee for service. Many family doctors have other pay arrangements, including salaries from a clinic or a health authority, and these types of arrangements have increased over time. In the case of alternative payment arrangements, doctors are encouraged to "shadow bill" — that is, to complete the billing claim form even though it is not required for payment. That way, it still enters the database.
6.   Lewchuk, Wayne, and Marlea Clarke. *Working Without Commitments: The Health Effects of Precarious Employment* (Montreal: McGill-Queen's University Press, 2011).
7.   Based on my unsystematic reading of Mincome files.
8.   Sarah Baird, Richard Garfein, Craig McIntosh and Berk Ozler, "Effect of a Cash Transfer Programme for Schooling on Prevalence of HIV and Herpes Simplex type 2 in Malawi: A Cluster Randomised Trial," *The Lancet* 379, no. 9823 (2012): 1320–29.
9.   Sarath Davala, Renana Jhabvala, Guy Standing, and Soumya Kapoor Mehta, *Basic Income: A Transformative Policy for India* (London: Bloomsbury, 2015).
10.   Andrea R. Ferro, Ana Lúcia Kassouf, and Deborah Levison, "The Impact of Conditional Cash Transfer Programs on Household Work Decisions in Brazil," in *Child Labor and the Transition between School and Work*, eds. Randall K.Q. Akee, Eric V. Edmonds, and Konstantinos Tatsiramos (Bingley, UK: Emerald Group Publishing Limited, 2010), 193–218.
11.   Translated from Nathalia Carvalho Moreira, Marco Aurelio Marques Ferreira, Alfonso Augusto Teixera de Freitas Carvalho, and Ivan Beck Ckagnazaroff, "Empoderamento das mulheres beneficiárias do Programa Bolsa Família na percepção dos agentes dos Centros de Referência de Assistência Social," *Revista de Administração Pública* 46, no. 2 (2012), 403–23.

Chapter 3

1.   Randy Fransoo, Patricia Martens, The Need To Know Team, Heather Prior, Charles Burchill, Ina Koseva, and Leanne Rajotte, *Who is in our Hospitals . . . And Why?* (Winnipeg, MB: Manitoba Centre for Health Policy, September 2013)
2.   Wilkins, R. 2007. *Mortality by Neighbourhood Income in Urban Canada from 1971 to 2001*. Ottawa: Statistics Canada, Health Analysis and Measurement Group.
3.   Data from 2006–2011. Winnipeg Regional Health Authority Community Health Assessments.
4.   Marni Brownell, Mariette Chartier, Rob Santos, Okechukwu Ekuma, Wendy Au, Joykrishna Sarkar, Leonard MacWilliam, Elaine Burland, Ina Koseva, and Wendy Guenette, *How Are Manitoba's Children Doing?* (Winnipeg, MB: Manitoba Centre for Health Policy, October 2012)
5.   Patricia Martens, Marni Brownell, Wendy Au, Leonard MacWilliam, Heather Prior, Jennifer Schultz, Wendy Guenette, Lawrence Elliott, Shelley Buchan, Marcia Anderson, Patricia Caetano, Colleen Metge, Rob Santos and Karen Serwonka, *Health Inequities in Manitoba: Is the Socioeconomic Gap Widening or Narrowing Over Time?* (Winnipeg, MB: Manitoba Centre for Health Policy, September 2010)

6. WHO [World Health Organization]. *The Economics of Social Determinants of Health and Health Inequalities: a resource book.* (WHO Press, 2013). http://apps.who.int/iris/bitstream/10665/84213/1/9789241548625_eng.pdf?ua=1&ua=1:, p. 6.

7. Public Health Agency of Canada, *Social Determinants of Health and Health Inequalities.* Date modified: 2018-06-13. http://www.phac-aspc.gc.ca/ph-sp/determinants/index-eng.php#key_determinants.

8. David Raphael, *Social Determinants of Health: Canadian Perspectives,* 2nd ed. (Toronto: Canadian Scholars' Press, 2009)

9. G. Dahlgren and M. Whitehead, *Policies and Strategies to Promote Social Equity in Health* (Stockholm: Institute for Futures Studies, 1991).

10. Valerie Tarasuk, "Implications of a Basic Income Guarantee for Household Food Insecurity." *Research Paper 24.* (Thunder Bay: Northern Policy Institute. June 2017). Retrieved from http://proof.utoronto.ca/.
    L. McIntyre, D.J. Dutton, C. Kwok, H.J. Emery. Reduction of Food Insecurity among Low-Income Canadian Seniors as a Likely Impact of a Guaranteed Annual Income. Canadian Public Policy 42: 3(2016): 274–286
    L. McIntyre. "Impact of a guaranteed annual income program on Canadian seniors' physical, mental and functional health." *Canadian Journal of Public Health,* 107:2(2016), p.E176.
    J. Lexchin, and P. Grootendorst, "Effects of prescription drug user fees on drug and health services use and on health status in vulnerable populations: a systematic review of the evidence." *International Journal of Health Services,* 34:1(2004), pp.101–122.

11. S. Cohen, D. Janicki-Deverts, W.J. Doyle, G.E. Miller, E. Frank, B.S. Rabin and R.B. Turner, "Chronic stress, glucocorticoid receptor resistance, inflammation, and disease risk. *Proceedings of the National Academy of Sciences,*" 109:16(2012), pp.5995–5999.
    E.S. Epel, E.H. Blackburn, J. Lin, F.S. Dhabhar, N.E. Adler, J.D. Morrow and R.M. Cawthon, "Accelerated telomere shortening in response to life stress." *Proceedings of the National Academy of Sciences of the United States of America,* 101:49(2004), pp.17312–17315.
    M.F. Marin, C. Lord, J. Andrews, R.P. Juster, S. Sindi, G. Arsenault-Lapierre, A.J. Fiocco and S.J. Lupien. "Chronic stress, cognitive functioning and mental health. *Neurobiology of learning and memory,*" 96:4(2011), pp.583–595.
    A. Steptoe and P.J. Feldman, "Neighborhood problem as sources of chronic stress: Development of a measure of neighborhood problems, and associations with socioeconomic status and health." *Annals of Behavioral Medicine.* August 2001, 23(3):177–185. 177–185.
    A. Baum, J. P. Garofalo and A.M. Yali, "Socioeconomic Status and Chronic Stress: Does Stress Account for SES Effects on Health?" Annals of the New York Academy of Sciences, 896 (1999): 131–144.

12. See: Richard G. Wilkinson and Kate Pickett, *The Spirit Level: Why Equality Is Better for Everyone* (London: Penguin, 2010). Some critics have argued that the observed results are not the result of inequality, but the authors and many others have provided compelling evidence. See:
    Kate E. Pickett and Richard G. Wilkinson, "Income Inequality and Health: a causal review." *Social Science & Medicine* 128 (2015): 316–326.

13. See: Richard G. Wilkinson and Kate Pickett, Income inequality and population health: a review and explanation of the evidence. *Soc. Sci. Med.* 62 (2006): 1768–1784
    Richard G. Wilkinson, *Unhealthy Societies: the Afflictions of Inequality* (Routledge: London, 1996).

14. Richard V. Reeves, *Dream Hoarders* (Washington: The Brookings Institution Press, 2017).
15. The comparison is between member countries of the Organisation for Economic Co-operation and Development. The raw US score fell by 0.51 (on a 10-point scale).
16. See: R. de Vries, S. Gosling, J. Potter, "Income inequality and personality: are less equal U.S. states less agreeable?" *Soc. Sci. Med.* 72(2011): 1978–1985.
    M. Paskov, C. Dewilde, Income inequality and solidarity in Europe. *Res. Soc. Stratif. Mobil.* 30(2012): 415–432.
    J. Helliwell, R. Layard, and J. Sachs, J. *World Happiness Report 2017* (New York: Sustainable Development Solutions Network, 2017).
17. The US Burden of Disease Collaborators, "The State of US Health, 1990–2016," *JAMA* 319, no. 14 (2018): 1444–72.

Chapter 4

1. "What billionaires and business titans say about cash handouts in 2017 (Hint: Lots!)": https://www.cnbc.com/2017/12/27/what-billionaires-say-about-universal-basic-income-in-2017.html.
2. https://www.cnbc.com/2017/08/16/billionaire-richard-branson-weighs-in-on-free-cash-handouts.html.
3. http://www.businessinsider.com/mark-zuckerberg-basic-income-harvard-speech-2017-5.
4. http://www.newsweek.com/stephen-hawking-wealth-redistribution-reddit-845497.
5. http://www.businessessinsider.com/sam-altman-basic-income-gdp-profit-sharing-2017-12.
6. Joel Lee, "Self Driving Cars Endanger Millions of American Jobs (And That's Okay)," *Mud*, June 19, 2015, http://www.makeuseof.com/tag/self-driving-cars-endanger-millions-american-jobs-thats-okay/ See also: Gao et al. 2016.
7. P. Godsmark, "Automated Vehicles: the coming of the next disruptive technology," *Conference Board of Canada.* January 2015. 8.   John Stuart Mill, *Principles of Political Economy with Some of their Applications to Social Philosophy*, book IV, chapter VI (London: 1848).
9. Ibid.
10. Adam Smith, *On the Wealth of Nations*, vol. 2 (Oxford: Clarendon Press, 1869 [1776]), 365.
11. See: C. Frey and M. Osborne, *The Future Of Employment: How Susceptible are Jobs to Computerization.* Oxford Martin School. September 17, 2013.
    http://www.oxfordmartin.ox.ac.uk/downloads/academic/future-of-employment.pdf
12. See: C. Lamb, *The Talented Mr. Robot: The Impact of Automation on Canada's Workforce.* Brookfield Institute for Innovation + Entrepreneurship. June 2016.
    http://brookfieldinstitute.ca/wp-content/uploads/2016/07/TheTalentedMrRobotReport.pdf.
13. Policy Horizons, *Canada and the Changing Nature of Work* (Ottawa: Government of Canada, 2016),
    http://www.horizons.gc.ca/sites/default/files/Publication-alt-format/2016-0265-eng.pdf.
14. See: A. McElvoy, M. Valencia, R. Avent, "Ireland's Forbidden Fruit." *The Economist*, August 30, 2016.
    http://www.economist.com/blogs/freeexchange/2016/08/money-talks-3.

Chapter 5

1. A prairie word: "dainties" are small cookies and squares, often frozen by home bakers to be thawed and served for company or at church luncheons.
2. John Helliwell, Richard Layard and Jeffrey Sachs, *World Happiness Report 2017* (New York: Sustainable Development Solutions Network, 2017).
3. "Affect" is a psychological term that describes how often people experience positive sensations, emotions and sentiments. Positive affect is associated with high energy, enthusiasm, activity and confidence; people with positive affect are often sociable, helpful and open-minded. Those with high negative affect are often distressed, sad, lethargic, anxious and depressed.
4. "Life evaluation" is a psychological term that measures how meaningful and satisfactory individuals find their lives.
5. Jonah N. Cohen, M. Taylor Dryman, Amanda Morrison, Kirsten Elizabeth Gilbert, Richard G. Heimberg and June Gruber, "Positive and Negative Affect as Links between Social Anxiety and Depression: Predicting Concurrent and Prospective Mood Symptoms in Unipolar and Bipolar Mood Disorders," *Behavior Therapy* 48, no. 6 (2017): 820–33, doi:10.1016/j.beth.2017.07.003. See also: Kristin Naragon and David Watson, "Positive affectivity," in *The Encyclopedia of Positive Psychology*, ed. Shane J. Lopez (Hoboken, NJ: Wiley-Blackwell, 2009), 701–11.
6. Maaike van der Noordt, Wilhelmina Ijzelenberg, Mariel Droomers and Karin Proper, "Health Effects of Employment: A Systematic Review of Prospective Studies," *Occupational and Environmental Medicine* 71, no. 10 (2014):730–36.
7. https://www.ted.com/talks/dan_ariely_what_makes_us_feel_good_about_our_work
8. Harold W. Watts and Albert Rees, eds., *The New Jersey Income-Maintenance Experiment*, vols. 2 & 3 (New York, Academic Press, 1977).
9. Gary Burtless and Jerry Hausman, "The Effect of Taxation on Labor Supply: Evaluating the Gary Negative Income Tax Experiment," *The Journal of Political Economy* 86, no. 6 (1978): 1103–30.
10. Robert A. Levine, Harold Watts, Robinson Hollister, Walter Williams, Alice O'Connor and Karl Widerquist, "A Retrospective on the Negative Income Tax Experiments: Looking Back at the Most Innovative Field Studies in Social Policy," in *The Ethics and Economics of the Basic Income Guarantee*, Karl Widerquist, Michael Anthony Lewis and Steven Pressman, eds. (Aldershot: Ashgate, 2005) 95–106.
11. Michael Hannan, Nancy Tuma and Lyle Groeneveld, "Income and Independence Effects on Marital Dissolution: Results from the Seattle and Denver Income-Maintenance Experiments," *American Journal of Sociology* 84, no. 3 (1978): 611–33.
12. Evelyn L. Forget, "The Town with No Poverty," *Canadian Public Policy* 37, no. 3 (2011): 283–305.
13. In 1974, as the Mincome experiment ramped up, the Canadian labour force participation rate for men aged twenty-five to fifty-four was 94.5 per cent while that for women was 48.3 per cent. Between 1975 and 1978, the period of active experimentation, the rate for women increased monotonically from 50.7 to 56.2 per cent while that for men fluctuated between 94.3 per cent and 94.6 per cent. By 2014, the participation rate for men fell to 90.5 per cent while that for women rose to 81.9 per cent.
14. Jitka Specianova, "Labor Supply Elasticity in the Unconditional Basic Income System: Data Sources and Methodological Issues," *European Scientific Journal* 14, no. 4 (2018).
15. Juliet B. Schor, *The Overworked American* (New York: Basic Books, 1992).

Chapter 6

1. See: Barbara R. Bergmann, Basic Income Grants or the Welfare State: Which Better Promotes Gender Equality? *Basic Income Studies*, 3 No. 3 (2008): pp. 1–7.
2. See: Sheila Regehr, *Basic Income and Gender Equality: Reflections on the Potential for Good Policy in Canada.* (2014) http://www.basicincome.org/bien/pdf/montreal2014/BIEN2014_Regehr.pdf
   Ailsa McKay, "Why a citizens' basic income? A question of gender equality or gender bias." *Work, Employment and Society* 21 No. 2(2007), pp.337–348.
   Carole Pateman, 2004. "Democratizing citizenship: some advantages of a basic income." *Politics & Society*, 32 No. 1(2004), pp.89–105.
4. See: Nancy Folbre, *The invisible heart: Economics and family values* (New Press, 2001).
5. See: Kathleen Lahey, K. Guaranteed Income Won't Help Women: Opinion. *The Star.* April 20, 2017. https://www.thestar.com/opinion/commentary/2017/04/20/guaranteed-income-wont-help-women-opinion.html.
6. http://www.statcan.gc.ca/daily-quotidien/170913/dq170913a-eng.htm.
7. http://www.statcan.gc.ca/daily-quotidien/170601/dq170601a-eng.htm.
8. Calculated based on 2015 data in "Changing Profile of Stay at Home Parents," *Statistics Canada*, 2017, and 2014 data in "Lone-parent Families," *Statistics Canada*, 2015.
9. See: B. Petersson, R. Mariscal, K. Ishi, K. Women Are Key for Future Growth: Evidence from Canada. *IMF Working Paper.* July 13, 2017. WP/17/166. http://www.imf.org/en/Publications/WP/Issues/2017/07/19/Women-Are-Key-for-Future-Growth-Evidence-from-Canada-45047.
10. See: J. Greenwood, N. Guner, G. Kocharkov and C. Santos, "Marry your like: Assortative mating and income inequality." *The American Economic Review*, 104 No. 5 (2014), pp.348–353.
11. A special issue of *Basic Income Studies* published in December 2008, entitled "Should Feminists Endorse Basic Income?" publishes alternative perspectives. www.bepress.com/bis/vol3/iss3.
12. "Average and median total income of husband-wife families," CANSIM Table 202-0105, *Statistics Canada.*
13. Low Income Measure, after tax. "Low income statistics by age, sex and family type," CANSIM Table 206-0041, *Statistics Canada.*
14. See: M. Moyser, Women and Paid Work. *Statistics Canada* 89-503X. March 9, 2017. http://www.statcan.gc.ca/pub/89-503-x/2015001/article/14694-eng.htm.
15. Low Income Measure, after tax. "Low income statistics by age, sex and family type," CANSIM Table 206-0041, *Statistics Canada.*

Chapter 7

1. As measured by the after-tax Low Income Measure.
2. 2016 Census.
3. Karl Widerquist and Michael W. Howard, eds., *Alaska's Permanent Fund Dividend: Examining its Suitability as a Model* (New York: Palgrave Macmillan, 2012). See also: Karl Widerquist and Michael W. Howard, eds., *Exporting the Alaska Model: Adapting the Permanent Fund Dividend for Reform around the World* (New York: Palgrave Macmillan, 2012).
4. According to the 2016 Census. http://behindthenumbers.ca/2017/10/27/population-changing-income-inequality-remains/.

5. Susan M. Sawyer, Peter S. Azzopardi, Dakshitha Wickremarathne and George C. Patton, "The Age of Adolescence," *The Lancet Child and Adolescent Health* 2 (2018): 223–28, doi: http://dx.doi.org/10.1016/S2352-4642(18)30022-1.

6. See, for example: G. Becker, *Human Capital: a theoretical and empirical analysis with special reference to education. 3rd edition* (National Bureau of Economic Research, 1994).
    A. Clark, Y. Georgellis, and P. Sanfey. "Scarring: The psychological impact of past Unemployment." *Economica* 68: 270 (2001): 221–241.
    G. Cruces, A. Ham and M. Viollaz. *Scarring effects of youth unemployment and informality. Evidence from Argentina and Brazil* (CEDLAS: Center for Distributive, Labor and Social Studies. Facultad de Ciencias Económicas Universidad Nacional de la Plata, 2012). http://www.iza.org/conference_files/YULMI2012/viollaz_m8017.pdf.
    P.-A. Edin and M. Gustavsson. 2008. "Time out of work and skill depreciation." *Industrial and Labor Relations Review* 61:2 (2008): 163–180.
    B. Lockwood. Information Externalities in the Labour Market and the Duration of Unemployment. *Review of Economic Studies* 58:4 (1991): 733–753.
    O. Nordstrom. *Scarring effects of the first labor market experience.* (Bonn: IZA Discussion Paper, No. 5565, 2011).
    C. Pissarides. Search unemployment with on-the-job search. *The Review of Economic Studies* 61:3 (1994): 457–475.

7. 2016 Census.

8. 2012 Canadian Survey on Disabilities.

9. Katherine Wall, *Insights on Canadian Society: Low Income Among Persons with a Disability in Canada* (Ottawa: Statistics Canada, 2017).

10. Michael Mendelson, Ken Battle, Sherry Torjman, and Ernie Lightman, *A Basic Income Plan for Canadians with Severe Disabilities* (Ottawa: Caledon Institute, 2010), http://www.ccdonline.ca/en/socialpolicy/poverty-citizenship/income-security-reform/basic-income-plan-for-canadians-with-severe-disabilities.

11. Lucie Dumais, Alexandra Prohet and Marie-Noëlle Ducharme in collaboration with Léonie Archambault and Maude Ménard-Dunn, *Review of Extra Costs Associated with Disability* (Montreal: UQAM, 2015), http://www.ccdonline.ca/en/socialpolicy/poverty-citizenship/income-security-reform/extra-costs-linked-to-disability.

Chapter 8

1. See: Milton Friedman, *Capitalism and freedom: with the assistance of Rose D. Friedman* (Chicago: University of Chicago Press, 1962).

2. See: Charles Lammam and Hugh McIntyre, *The Practical Challenges of Creating a Guaranteed Annual Income* (Vancouver: Fraser Institute, 2015).

3. The comparable rates for persons with disabilities are $16,920 and $13,934, and for a single mother with a two-year-old $24,162 and $18,854. See: A. Tweddle, K. Battle, S. Torjman. Welfare in Canada 2013 (Caledon Institute. November, 2014), App. B1.

4. David Calnitsky, "The Employer Response to the Guaranteed Annual Income," *Socio-Economic Review* (2018), doi: 10.1093/ser/mwy009.

5. I'm not sure the employers were correct about the causation. They knew Mincome was underway, so it was easy to blame the program for wage increases. However, the 1970s were a time of significant wage inflation across the country. I suspect higher wages had more to do with general trends than with Mincome.

6. For a discussion of the politics surrounding Family Allowances, see N. Christie.

Engendering the State: Family, Work, and Welfare in Canada (Toronto: University of Toronto Press, 2000).

7.   See: Hugh Grant *W.A. Mackintosh: The Life of a Canadian Economist* (Montreal: McGill-Queen's University Press, 2015), footnote 53.

8.   Michael A. Clemens, "Does Kicking Out Mexicans Create Jobs?" *Politico Magazine*, February 15, 2017, https://www.politico.com/magazine/story/2017/02/mexico-immigrant-workers-jobs-americans-braceros-history-immigration-214784.

9.   Alex Himmelfarb and Roy Romanow, "We can end homelessness in Canada," *The Globe and Mail*, January 16, 2017 [updated March 21, 2018] https://www.theglobeandmail.com/opinion/we-can-end-homelessness-in-canada/article33632029/.

10. See: Alex Smith and Nasraddine Ammar, "Costing a National Guaranteed Basic Income Using the Ontario Basic Income Model," *Parliamentary Budget Office Blog*, April 17, 2018. http://www.pbo-dpb.gc.ca/en/blog/news/Guaranteed_Basic_Income.

11. There is an extensive history of the development of active labour market policies from the 1950s to the present in: Weishaupt, T. *From the Manpower Revolution to the Activation Paradigm: Explaining Institutional Continuity and Change in an Integrating Europe*, (Amsterdam: Amsterdam University Press, 2011).

12. See: OECD, *Society at a Glance 2016: OECD Social Indicators*, OECD Publishing, Paris. http://dx.doi.org/10.1787/9789264261488-en.

13. See: J.P. Martin, *Activation and Active Labour Market Policies in OECD Countries: Stylized Facts and Evidence on Their Effectiveness*. IZA Discussion Paper No. 84. (2014) http://ftp.iza.org/pp84.pdf.

14. See: J. Rothstein, "Is the EITC as good as an NIT? Conditional cash transfers and tax incidence." *American Economic Journal: Economic Policy*, 2 No. 1(2010), pp.177–208.

15. See: Stephenson Strobel and E.L. Forget. Revitalizing poverty reduction and social inclusion. *Manitoba Law Journal*. 37 No. 2 (2015): 259–276.

Chapter 9

1.   Parliamentary Budget Office. "Costing a National Guaranteed Basic Income Using the Ontario Basic Income Model." April 17, 2018. http://www.pbo-dpb.gc.ca/web/default/files/Documents/Reports/2018/Basic%20Income/Basic_Income_Costing_EN.pdf.

2.   It should be a simple matter to determine how much each province pays for income assistance, but that is not the case. These data are typically aggregated with other provincial programs in published data, and administrative costs are rarely identified with particular programs. In the past, the National Council on Welfare tracked provincial income assistance expenditure, but that body was disbanded in 2012. John Stapleton has picked up the mantle and estimates a total cost for Canada of nineteen billion dollars in 2017, not including administrative costs.

3.   The Canadian Association of Social Workers estimated the combined costs of federal, provincial and municipal governments for income assistance at more than $185 billion (CASW, 2017). The Parliamentary Budget Office estimate, adjusted for provincial income assistance, is remarkably close to the net cost I estimated in Evelyn L. Forget, *Is a Basic Income Guarantee Still Relevant in Canada?* (Thunder Bay: Northern Policy Institute, 2017).

4.   Richard Pereira, "The Cost of Universal Basic Income: Public Savings and Program Redundancy Exceed Cost," in *Financing Basic Income* (New York: Springer International, 2017), 9–45.

5.   See, for example: Dan Ariely, *Predictably Irrational. The Hidden Forces That Shape Our*

Decisions (New York: HarperCollins, 2008).

6. See: Kevin Milligan. "Everyone is talking about Basic Income. Here's Why they Don't Do It" *Globe and Mail*, December 12, 2015, https://www.theglobeandmail.com/report-on-business/rob-commentary/everyone-talks-about-basic-income-heres-why-they-dont-implement-it/article27723204/; Kevin Milligan, "Dare to Dream but Do the Math," blog post, July 4, 2016, https://www.cdhowe.org/intelligence-memos/kevin-milligan-dare-dream-do-math. See also: Jonathan Rhys Kesselman, "A Dubious Antipoverty Strategy: Guaranteeing Incomes for the Poor Is Politically Unfeasible and Financially Unsustainable," *Inroads* 34 (2014): 33–43, http://inroadsjournal.ca/a-dubious-antipoverty-strategy/http://inroadsjournal.ca/a-dubious-antipoverty-strategy/http://inroadsjournal.ca/a-dubious-antipoverty-strategy/.

7. Andrew Coyne, "Three Points on the GST to End Poverty?" *National Post*, April 18, 2018, http://nationalpost.com/opinion/andrew-coyne-three-points-on-the-gst-to-end-poverty-guaranteed-income-sounds-like-a-good-deal.

8. See: Michael T. Hannan, Nancy Brandon Tuma and Lyle P. Groeneveld. "Income and Independence Effects on Marital Dissolution: Results from the Seattle and Denver Income-Maintenance Experiments." *American Journal of Sociology* 84, no. 3 (1978): 611–33.

9. See: Daniel P. Moynihan, *The politics of a guaranteed income: The Nixon administration and the family assistance plan* (Vintage Books, 1973).

10. See: G.G. Cain and D.A. Wissoker, "A Reanalyis of Marital Stability in the Seattle-Denver Income-Maintenance Experiment," *American Journal of Sociology* 95, no. 5 (March 1990): 1235–1269.

11. Thanks to Harvey Stevens for the estimate.

Chapter 10

1. Measured, for example, by real GDP per capita. A basic income that grows by the rate of increase of nominal GDP over time will protect payments from inflation and share the benefits of growth.

2. Virginia Eubanks, "The Digital Poorhouse," *Harper's Magazine*, January, 2018, 12.

Appendix

1. Including the federal Working Income Tax Benefit and provincial programs in New Brunswick, Quebec, Alberta and B.C.

2. Robin W. Boadway, Katherine Cuff and Kourtney Koebel, "Designing a Basic Income Guarantee for Canada" (Kingston ON: Queen's University Economics Dept. No. 1371, 2016).

3. Derek Hum and Wayne Simpson, "The Cost of Eliminating Poverty in Canada: Basic Income with an Income Test Twist," in K. Widerquist, M. Lewis and S. Pressman (eds.), *The Ethics and Economics of the Basic Income Guarantee* (Aldershot, UK: Ashgate, 2005), 282–92.

    Margot Young and James P. Mulvale, *Possibilities and Prospects: The Debate over a Guaranteed Income* (Ottawa: Canadian Centre for Policy Alternatives, 2009).

    Harvey Stevens and Wayne Simpson "Toward a National Universal Guaranteed Basic Income." *Canadian Public Policy*, 43 No. 2 (2017), pp.120-139.

    C. Lammam and H. McIntyre, *The Practical Challenges of Creating a Guaranteed Annual Income in Canada* (Vancouver: Fraser Institute, January 2015).

Index

United States 11, 36, 38, 57–61, 67, 85–87, 130, 140–41, 154, 157, 166, 172–73, 177, 182, 186

V

volunteering 11, 23, 33, 68, 82–83, 92, 94, 108, 117–19, 125, 141, 175

W

welfare 21–22, 35, 37, 40, 60, 121, 141, 165, 173, 183, 187, 199

well-being 22, 30–31, 33, 41, 58–61, 78–83, 91–93, 100, 107, 125, 167, 174

Winnipeg, MB 10, 13, 23, 36, 39, 41–42, 48, 51, 78, 85–86

women 14, 34, 38, 51, 48, 71, 82, 88–89, 96–106, 108–12, 157, 184, 187, 189, 203

work

demand for 18, 31, 65–76, 130–131, 134, 138, 144–46

for a living 10–11, 13–14, 22, 79–80, 92–93, 96, 130–31

full-time 17, 27, 29, 75–77, 81–82, 88, 102, 154, 156, 159

hours 9, 13, 32–33, 64, 71, 80, 83–84, 85–91, 96, 188–89

part–time 17–19, 29, 31, 75–76, 82, 117, 154, 156, 184

reasons people 80–84, 87, 90, 92–96, 130–31, 154–55

World Bank 11, 166

World Health Organization 52

Y

young people 14–15, 19, 21, 35, 37, 76, 91, 111, 116–19, 125, 138, 143, 158–59